Emerson's First Marriage

EMERSON'S
FIRST MARRIAGE

Henry F. Pommer

Carbondale and Edwardsville

SOUTHERN ILLINOIS UNIVERSITY PRESS

FEFFER & SIMONS, INC.

London and Amsterdam

Preface

Emerson's most dramatic acts, most influential writing, and most profound sorrows came during the fifteen years between his twenty-fourth and thirty-ninth birthdays; these are the years most important to an understanding of the man and the thinker. At the close of this period, which ended with the death of his son, Waldo, Emerson wrote that

> *this losing is true dying;*
> *This is lordly man's down-lying, . . .*
> *Star by star his world resigning.*

Eleven years earlier, his first wife's star had already set. Their marriage and her death were the first dramatic episode and the first tragedy of the fifteen-year period.

New details of the courtship and marriage enriched Ralph L. Rusk's edition of Emerson's letters in 1939 and his definitive biography ten years later. In 1962 the publication of Ellen Tucker's letters released further documents concerning her and Waldo's engagement. Additional letters of the Emerson family have been available in manuscript for this study. Consequently, as many significant data as will probably ever be discovered now reveal what kind of woman won the young minister's love, and what the relationship between them was.

In learning and telling their story I have had the generous help of Allegheny College through a sabbatic leave and several travel grants; of the Ralph Waldo Emerson Memorial Association, which has allowed quotation from unpublished documents deposited by it in the Houghton Library of Harvard University; of Miss Carolyn Jakeman of the Houghton Library; and of the staff of Reis Library of Allegheny College. Dr. Ethel Emerson Wortis, descendant of Emerson's brother William, has permitted me to quote from her collection of unpublished family correspondence; Mrs. Edith W. Gregg, great-granddaughter of Emerson and editor of Ellen Tucker's letters, read my manuscript carefully and saved me from several errors; Mr. and Mrs. Robert Beyer were generous hosts in their home, formerly owned by Colonel William A. Kent in Concord, New Hampshire; Professor and Mrs. Richard Hutcheson made valuable suggestions about the text. My wife receives my warmest thanks for research assistance, constant encouragement, helpful criticism, and the blessing of a home where study and writing are a delight.

Readers disappointed by the lack of references to other biographers will find compensation in the Appendix.

H.F.P.

Meadville, Pennsylvania
February, 1967

Contents

Ralph Waldo Emerson
A Brief Chronology

1803	Birth of Ralph Waldo Emerson, in Boston, Massachusetts.
1811	Death of his father, William Emerson.
1821	Graduation, A.B., from Harvard.
1821–1828	Alternation of teaching school, and studying divinity at Harvard.
1827, December	First visit to Concord, New Hampshire, where he met Ellen Louisa Tucker.
1828, December	Engagement of Waldo and Ellen.
1829, March	Ordination as junior pastor of the Second Church, Boston.
1829, September	Marriage to Ellen.
1830, March to May	Ellen's trip to Philadelphia.
1831, February	Death of Ellen.
1832, September	Resignation from the Second Church.
1832, November	Death of Margaret Tucker, Ellen's sister.
1832, December	Departure for first visit to Europe.
1833, February	Death of Mrs. Kent, Ellen's mother.
1834	Transfer to Waldo of a large part of Ellen's estate.
1835	Marriage to Lydia Jackson.
1836	Publication of *Nature,* his first book.
1839	Birth of Ellen Tucker Emerson.
1842	Death of Waldo, his first son.
1847	Second visit to Europe.
1882	Death, in Concord, Massachusetts.
1892	Death of Lydia (Lidian) Emerson.

Emerson's First Marriage

ONE

Dangerous Neighborhood

"Hast no curiosity to see the Beauty of the world?
the diamond idea that illuminates my retirements
& rejoices my intercourse or if that is poor
English—makes my society."

Emerson to his brother William, March 6, 1829.

DURING the latter half of 1827, Ralph Waldo Emerson was studying theology at Harvard and from time to time preaching in Unitarian pulpits. His home was Divinity Hall, for his family had very limited resources and no home of its own. The mother, Ruth Haskins Emerson, had been a widow sixteen years and was currently living in Concord, Massachusetts, with her husband's step-father, the Reverend Ezra Ripley. Her oldest son, William, was studying law in New York; Edward had just been graduated from Harvard and was also studying law, with Daniel Webster; Bulkeley, mentally retarded, was cared for by a rural family; Charles, the youngest, was a Harvard undergraduate.[1]

Waldo—as he was then called—recorded in his journal that he had never been in love,[2] though five years earlier he had felt love's beginning, partly because of a woman "known and to be known." [3] During 1824 he had recognized

a signal defect of character which neutralizes in great part the just influence my talents ought to have. . . . Its bitter fruits are a sore uneasiness in the company of most men & women, a frigid fear of offending & jealousy of disrespect . . . which contrive to make me second with all those among whom chiefly I wish to be first.

He quoted with approval Juvenal's question whether a man intending marriage were being driven mad by snakes, but was unable to believe that folly in matrimony was "always or generally the case." He wrote that Beauty "sends its dart / Thro' skin blood & bone to the core of the heart," and believed that "ambition & curiosity" would prompt a person like himself

to prove by experiments the affections & faculties. . . . You will bind yourself in friendship; you will obey the strong necessity of Nature and knit yourself to woman in love. & the exercise of these affections will open your apprehension to a more common feeling & closer kindred with men.

Though he had not yet loved, he was far from being a misogynist.[4]

By 1827 a daily stage had for years been linking Boston with Concord, New Hampshire—"New Concord," that is, about sixty miles north of "Old Concord" in Massachusetts.[5] Towards the end of December, Waldo made the trip in order to preach in New Concord twice on each of three Sundays and once on Christmas.[6] He went with some regrets, for only two days after he had agreed to fill the pulpit at Concord he received a similar invitation from Brighton—an invitation he preferred because it would have permitted him to continue in Divinity Hall. But if the invitation from Brighton had come earlier, he might never have been linked to the "diamond chain" of Ellen Louisa Tucker.[7]

In his journal and letters he recorded much of his three-week visit in New Hampshire. Its Concord could not, in his judgment, "compare with the Old. The village is large [;] the street I suppose is a mile long, and the population perhaps 3500. The Unitarian Society is small & meets for public worship in the Court House, but . . . design to build a meeting house in the Spring." After two weeks he found his stay "a pretty long one. I get no letters, though I plague the Postmaster, from either of my busy brothers. Fortunately I stocked my trunk with books." He planned to join a sleighing party to the Shaker Society at nearby Canterbury;[8] he visited the prison and thought that the fifteen hours convicts spent locked in their cells each day must be dreadful.[9] What he did not record at the time is that on Christmas Day, 1827, he first saw Ellen.[10]

Although a single circumstance had taken him to Concord, a network determined that once there he must meet her. She was a stepdaughter of one of the town's most prominent citizens, Colonel

William A. Kent. Retired from business by 1806, he had been Treasurer of the State from 1814 to 1816.[11] A widower in 1821, he married in that year Margaret, widow of Bezaleel Tucker of Boston, who had left considerable property to his wife and children.[12] The resulting family was, as Waldo remarked, not only large but respectable.[13] Colonel Kent had entertained President Monroe in 1817, and Lafayette only two years before Emerson. Daniel Webster was a frequent visitor; a young minister would have been asked to dine too, even if it had not been the case that Colonel Kent's fourth son, Edward, had been one of Waldo's classmates and admirers at Harvard.[14] Finally, the entire family was, in Waldo's words, "the most forward in the establishment of the new church." [15]

Years later Emerson spoke fondly of "the first smile of Ellen on the door stone at Concord." [16] In 1827, she was sixteen; [17] he, twenty-four. Perhaps she had already been predisposed towards him by Edward's enthusiasm and by the pre-Christmas sermon in which Waldo stressed the importance of being virtuous within our homes where "by the strong cords of friendship and love" God "invested the fireside with its sacred delights." [18]

- 2 -

NO CORRESPONDENCE between Ellen and Waldo, and none in which either mentions the other, has survived from the twelve months following their

Christmas meeting. We must imagine the emotions of that year largely by the light of its public events.

At the close of that Christmas visit to New Concord in 1827, Waldo returned to his studies at Harvard, wrote "something less than a sermon a month," and husbanded his delicate strength. Several churches asked him to candidate in their pulpits, but he did not feel strong enough to do so. He did obligate himself to six Sundays' preaching in New Concord beginning May 25,[19] but a few days after the series began he was summoned to Old Concord by an illness of his brother Edward.[20] He returned to New Hampshire on June 10, but was back in Cambridge by the end of the month.[21] Behind him he left a "constantly increasing" church which through one of Ellen's stepbrothers urged that the American Unitarian Association send Emerson back for a longer stay. But he had committed himself to supplying the pulpit of the Second Church (Old North) in Boston; its distinguished minister, Henry Ware, Jr., was ill and for an indefinite period would be unable to preach. In October this continuing commitment prevented Waldo's accepting even a short-term invitation from the Reverend Moses G. Thomas, provisionally attached to Ellen's church.[22]

Soon, however, two circumstances combined to make his absence from Boston desirable. First, Mr. Ware was planning to resign; many members of the church wanted to employ Emerson, but Waldo was anxious that the congregation hear other candidates before making up its mind. Second, Edward had been in the Charlestown Asylum; although he was much improved, it seemed wise that Waldo take him on a short trip before returning him to Old Concord. Where should they go?

Waldo knew that Ellen's Concord was for him a "dangerous neighborhood," [23] and in his journal he noted that

it is hard to yoke love & wisdom. It is hard to criticize the behavior of Beauty. In her magic presence, reason becomes ashamed of himself & wears the aspect of Pedantry or Calculation. Sentiment triumphs, . . . quotes triumphantly the ancient theory (a sweet falsehood) that Beauty is the flower of Virtue. Experience looks grave & . . . musters his saws, . . . &, what he chiefly relies on, the impressions formerly made on the same heart by other & loftier qualities which reason and stoicism justified. A pretty plea, no doubt, but if the Daemon of the man should throw him into circumstances favorable to the sentiment, reason would stand on a perilous . . . footing. The terms of intercourse in society are singularly unpropitious to the virtuous curiosity of young men with regard to the inner qualities of a beautiful woman. They may only see the outside of the house they want to buy. The chance is very greatly against her possessing those virtues & general principles which they most value.[24]

Believing that he had overcome his "blushes & wishes," he left with Edward for New Concord on the sixth of December.[25] But he had purchased one of the saccharine anthologies or gift books popular at the time—this one entitled *Forget Me Not* and bought "for ELT." [26]

Waldo preached at least two sermons on each of the three Sundays of this visit.[27] On the tenth of December he wrote a long, cheerful, chatty letter to Charles, but with no mention of Ellen or hint of romance.[28] Probably within a day or two he and Ellen had their first serious interview, and Emerson described his prospects. Ellen replied, "I do not wish to hear of your prospects." After all, she had money of her own.[29]

She also had beauty. To his brother William, Waldo described himself as having been "overthrown by the eye & ear": Ellen was "very beautiful." Later he added that she was "perfectly simple though very elegant in her manners." [30] Less biased testimony comes from surviving portraits of Ellen; they show her with a full bust, dark eyes, high forehead, dark hair symmetrically arranged in numerous tight curls, long nose, small mouth and chin, and an expression of alertness and charm.[31] Although Emerson thought one of these portraits very inaccurate, Edward thought it "nearly perfect." [32] Charles remembered her "unstudied dignity of mien & air," and thought her "an Ideal that, if I were a Platonist, I should believe to have been one of the Forms of Beauty in the Universal Mind." [33] "Very beautiful" was also the judgment of Waldo's more distant relatives and of his parishioners.[34]

She had had other suitors, yet none as attractive as Waldo. As for him, ten days of her allied charms vanquished his experience and reason. On December 17, 1828, they were formally en-

gaged.[35] Waldo is said to have announced the fact
at his boardinghouse with great frankness and
ingenuousness, whereupon a fellow boarder "gave
utterance to the exuberance of his feeling by saying, 'Let us join in singing,—*Blest are the sons of
peace* . . .'" [36]

Altogether Waldo had spent, since their meeting, about forty-three days in New Concord—not
every one of them necessarily with Ellen. To her
it seemed that they had been acquainted only two
weeks—though she felt she had already loved him
six months. The days were past when she could
think of herself as "a solitary thing" as "respects
. . . those of my own age and standing."[37]

- *3* -

SHORTLY AFTER his engagement Waldo prayed in
his journal,

Will my Father in Heaven regard us with kindness, and
as he hath, as we trust, made us for each other, will he be
pleased to strengthen & purify & prosper & eternize our
affection! [38]

On the same day he read to Ellen's church a sermon which said in part that love "was a necessity;
but it was not the body but the spiritual properties
that we loved. The affections . . . tended to expect perfection in the loved person, and from
seeking perfection in the human friend were led to
seek it in God." [39]

A few more days, and he was back in Cambridge, buying Ellen another gift book (this one
including two poems and an allegory by him),

writing love poems, and telling the family his good fortune. Edward already knew, of course, and was "very highly gratified." [40] Charles wrote to William,

I have thought of the matter as coolly as I could, & it seems to me I shall never be so happy again, till I am engaged myself. We have not yet seen the fair nonpareil. . . . But charming surely she must be, to have engaged the affections of one whose eye is so quick & classical, whose judgment is so deliberate & whose demands on human nature are so large. We all rejoice at it.[41]

Though Waldo's letters were even more enthusiastic, they were also tinged by a fear not of Ellen, but of Fate. In late December the feeling was no more than that he was "as happy as it is safe in life to be." [42] Two weeks later it had grown—or was at least more fully expressed—in a letter to Aunt Mary Moody Emerson surveying the state of all five brothers.

You know—none can know better—on what straitened lines we have all walked up to manhood. In poverty and many troubles the seeds of our prosperity were sown. . . .
    Now look at the altered aspect. William has begun to live by the law. Edward has recovered his reason and his health. Bulkeley was never more comfortable in his life. Charles is prospering in all ways. Waldo is comparatively well and comparatively successful—far more so than his friends, out of his family, anticipated. Now I add to all this felicity a particular felicity which makes my own glass very much larger and fuller. And I straightway say, Can this hold? . . . There's an apprehension of reverse always arising from success. . . . The way to be safe is to be thankful. I cannot find in the world without, or within, any antidote, any bulwark, against this fear like this,—the frank acknowledgement of unbounded dependence.[43]

Additional happiness and success came within a few days: Ellen and her family moved to Boston for the rest of the winter, and by an overwhelming vote "an ancient & respectable church"—the Second—called Waldo to become the colleague and eventual successor of Henry Ware.[44] The two young people went briefly to Old Concord, where Ellen won the immediate love of Waldo's mother and of Mr. Ripley; but the return trip was in the rain.[45] On January 19 Ellen was "attacked with a bleeding at the lungs," and Waldo began paying the "fatal tax" for his well-being.[46]

Evidence of consumption was not new either within Ellen's family, nor to Ellen herself. Her father had experienced similar attacks; her only brother, traveling for his health at age twenty-two, had died of "a horrid cold"; her sister Margaret had "been raising blood" the summer before Ellen and Waldo met; and at about the same time something of the sort had happened to Ellen.[47]

The Emerson family history was equally discouraging. Several years before his death of a tumor, Waldo's father had suffered "a profuse hemorrhage from the lungs, from the effects of which he never completely recovered." An older brother of Waldo's died, while a child, of lung disease. Waldo himself went to South Carolina and then on to Florida for several months of 1826–27 because trouble with breathing made a northern winter dangerous.[48] During that trip he wrote to William, "I have but a single complaint,—a certain stricture on the right side of the chest, which always makes itself felt when the air is cold or damp, & the attempt to preach or like exertion of the lungs is followed by an aching." In February of 1828, two months after he had met Ellen, he told William, "I am living cautiously yea treading on eggs to strengthen my constitution. It is a long battle this of mine betwixt life & death & tis wholly uncertain to whom the game belongs." [49]

That Waldo recognized the seriousness of Ellen's symptoms is suggested by his saying to Charles within a day or two of her attack that "she is too lovely to live long. . . . Should she be struck out of existence tomorrow, it would still have been a rich blessing to have been permitted to have loved her." But his own apparent recovery gave Waldo reason to hope that Ellen might respond to "medicine & care so entirely, that she shall not be exposed to attacks . . . in the future." [50] No doubt his love helped him to overestimate her strength, but professional medical opinion was also encouraging. Ellen's physician from at least this time onward was Doctor James Jackson, research scientist and Harvard professor, who had cared for Edward Emerson. Because of Ellen, Waldo delayed answering the call to the Second Church until a conference with Doctor Jackson encouraged him to accept. [51]

- *4* -

ELLEN'S HEALTH did improve constantly during the next five months, and she and Waldo were able to see each other frequently. [52] In private, he wrote more love poetry; in public, he entered into the responsibilities of his pastorate.[53] His ordination was on March 11; Ellen was apparently not sufficiently recovered to attend, but the marshals reserved a pew for her mother and Waldo's, and Mrs. Emerson took "tea with her daughter intended." The service was moving, but Mr. Ware's health was an overshadowing cause for anxiety.[54] At the end of April, Ellen left for New Concord by way of Hartford and Worcester.[55]

In the middle of June, Waldo too left for New Hampshire—"to see the Seasons" he told Charles, who knew perfectly well that "there are fairer flowers than those of the field." [56] There was also an obligation to preach two Sundays in New Concord.[57] Ellen had been importuning him to come. She was well, riding horseback, obviously extremely happy in her love.[58] It should have been a gay visit, but on June 18, as Waldo wrote to Charles,

Ellen was taken sick in the old way,—very suddenly, & suffered in the night great distress, but the quantity of blood raised has not been much & some symptoms her mother says are much less unfavorable than at former times—but tis bad enough at the best & has wonderfully changed my visit. I was perfectly happy [;] now I am watching & fearing & pitied. . . .

Ellen has an angel's soul & tho very skeptical about the length of her own life hath a faith as clear & strong as those do that have Gods kingdom within them.

Because there was no competent physician in New Concord, Waldo wrote to Doctor Jackson,[59] and one wonders whether the latter, or anyone else, noticed that Ellen's first attack since her acquaintance with Waldo had occurred soon after their reunion in Boston, and the second immediately after their reunion in Concord. Was being with her fiancé more strain than she could stand? That such was the case finds confirmation in her remarks, during the recuperation of July, that she was not yet strong enough to see him.[60] Yet there was not always danger in their being together, for by early August, Ellen was so much recovered that she and Waldo set out in a chaise for the Shaker colony at Canterbury, resolved to go no farther if she did not benefit from that twelve-mile ride. She bore it so well, however, that the trip was extended nine or ten days; Waldo was convinced that in spite of rough roads "the journey is excellent for Ellen & so much better than her nurse & little hot chamber at home."

Their route was from Canterbury to Meredith Bridge, Centre Harbour, Tamworth, Conway, Bartlett, Plymouth, Orford, and Hanover; Waldo made a side trip to Crawford Notch.[61] They amused themselves with a rhyming journal such as Waldo had kept during his trip to Florida.[62] Mrs. Kent was their chaperone, but traveled—hardly to their great regret—in a separate vehicle with the baggage. Waldo disliked being away from the Second Church, where he was now the only active pastor and had recently received an increase of salary from $1200 to $1800; but he regarded his absence as "a duty of impossible omission," and made arrangements for a supply preacher, "with the less hesitation, that I do not expect to be absent in the fall for any island expedition." [63]

Probably it was during this trip that the two of them decided they would like a September wedding. In her first letter after Waldo had returned to Boston, Ellen wrote metaphorically, "We have tried a short journey together and like [it] so well that we think of taking a *longer.*" This and other letters now contained allusions to some "ugly subject"—probably her will—on which Waldo wanted Mrs. Kent to write to Pliny Cutler, Ellen's guardian and the executor of her father's estate. Concord gossip began to anticipate a wedding, and Colonel Kent had to be persuaded to do something—just what is not clear—but it may have been either to withdraw opposition to a fall wedding, or to agree that he and his wife, with Ellen's sisters Margaret and Paulina, should live with or close to the newlyweds in Boston. Ellen was very anxious to have her family near Waldo and herself.[64] Mr. Ware was still ailing, but no doubt Waldo had not only his colleague's health in mind when he wrote that "it is really good ground to hope that he has no seated consumption . . . if after so long an interval he remains as well."

In mid-September there was another ten-day trip that benefitted Ellen's health—to Merimack, Worcester, Springfield (where Waldo preached "all day"), Hartford, Vernon, Stafford Springs, and again Worcester. This time both Margaret and Mrs. Kent were in the second carriage. Lamb's *Essays of Elia,* Waldo reported to Charles, "is a very good book on a journey. . . . We have 6 vols of new novels &c beside & a couple of octavos. And we botanize & criticise & poetize & memorize & prize & grow wise we hope." [65]

On the thirtieth of September, 1829, they were married.[66]

The Reverend Mr. Thomas, who would soon be ordained as minister of the New Concord Unitarian Church and would become a year later another of Colonel Kent's sons-in-law, performed the ceremony in the north parlor of the Colonel's home.[67] The house in which so much of the courting had occurred and in which the marriage took place is still occupied, though on a new site. It is large, with four principal rooms on each of the first two floors, and a generous wing of smaller rooms.[68] Charles was the only one of Waldo's brothers present for the ceremony.[69] His record—written to William—revealed his own mood as much as anything else.

Ellen looked very well, & beautiful exceedingly. But commiserate me—you who tasted, I'm thinking, a grain of the lump I had to swallow. 3 whole days in that big house full of women, sat I, putting all the time a sober face on the fool's errand I went to do, while W. & the fair Ellen were whispering honied words above stairs, & I was turned over to the compulsory attentions of the stranger folk. These lovers are blind. . . . I forgive them freely.[70]

TWO

Queen and King

"I would draw characters [,] not write lives.
I would evoke the spirit of each and their relics
might rot."

Emerson's Journal for August 12, 1832.

WHENEVER the nine months of their engagement found them in different cities, Ellen and
Waldo corresponded briskly; at one period she
wrote every other day, and his letters appear to
have been almost as frequent. She asked that he
"not leave off writing me when we live together—I
love such long lived lines of affection";[1] but of
course marriage did halt their correspondence except during a brief separation in the spring of
1830. Indeed, more than three-quarters of all Ellen's extant letters are from the period of engagement. The whole of her correspondence, with the
comments made about her at various times by
other persons, reveal a character not subtle or
profound—she was only seventeen—but affection-

ate and virtuous, religious and intelligent, poetic, courageous, and gay.

It is clear that in New Concord Ellen lived in a very congenial household, and through her marriage merely enlarged the circle of those who loved her and whom she loved. The Kent and Tucker children lived together happily, nursing Ellen when she was ill, riding with her when she was well. Cousins visited, and friends dropped in for music and conversation. Colonel Kent, something of an invalid and reputedly taciturn,[2] was a loving tease to his stepdaughter, and when, after the engagement, a new room was added to the house, Ellen was allowed to have it so she could be alone. When marriage was about to take her away from New Concord, she hoped, as has been said, to move her family with her.[3]

She was always on equally affectionate terms with Waldo's relatives. Two of his brothers, his mother, stepgrandfather, and Aunt Mary have left evidence of their fondness for her. She responded in kind, writing warm notes to the brothers, making watch guards for Charles and William,[4] delighting to meet Grandfather Ripley, correspond with Aunt Mary, and entertain them in her home.[5] But of course Waldo had the largest share of her heart. She loved to hear him, see him, read his letters, think of him, pray for him. As the culture of that time would lead us to expect, she never so much as alluded to any type of physical contact, even leaning on his arm or kissing. Such mores and perhaps the weakness of her health

excluded from the whole record any mention of
the possibility or desirability of having children.

Prominent among her virtues was a desire for
spiritual improvement. She recognized faults in
herself such as being sometimes "disagreeable to
others and vastly uncomfortable" to herself, and
believed that after their marriage Waldo's daily
example would help her.[6] She wished always to be
perfectly frank with him about her shortcomings,
and was markedly grateful for well-being in general and for particular blessings—especially for
what she called their "golden courtship." [7] By a
curious coincidence, a physician read to Aunt
Mary a letter from his sister praising the character of a young woman who turned out to be Ellen
Tucker.[8] Waldo, of course, iterated such praise,
revealing the strongly ethical, nontheological
strain of his thought: "she is good,—& has character enough to be religious." [9]

Denominational harmony was undoubtedly
pleasant. Colonel Kent and at least one of his sons
were loyal Unitarians; Ellen was the first person
to join their church after the eight original members had established the covenant.[10] She gave the
society a ten-piece communion set—still in existence—little realizing that Waldo would resign his
pastorate of the Second Church in a disagreement
over communion ritual.[11]

Yet the religious bond between Waldo and
Ellen ran also to deeper levels. Her verses give
frequent evidence of piety, and her letters both
quote and allude to the Bible. Otherwise she made
few protestations of faith; we learn of it often

from persons around her, but she seems to have
been free of self-righteousness and religiosity.
More by what she did not say than by what she
did, we would know even without the record of
her membership that her sympathies were Unitarian rather than Congregational: religion seems
to have been for her chiefly a matter of gratitude
for God's blessings, petitionary prayers, an oft-
repeated faith in immortality, and benevolent actions among relatives, friends, and the poor of
New Concord.[12] When in later years Waldo wrote
"Spiritual Laws," he was obviously not describing
himself in the passage concerning a scholar who
"follows some giddy girl, not yet taught by religious passion to know the noble woman with all
that is serene, oracular and beautiful in her
soul." [13] Equally obviously, Ellen was equipped to
obey the injunction laid on her by Aunt Mary:
"Lean not on . . . [Waldo] for resources—but
urge him on to aid in the work of moral improvement which is going on for Heaven. Be yourself a
ministering angel to him and society." [14]

Ellen also showed worldly common sense and a
love of nature. Waldo ascribed the former to
her, and it must have appealed to him with his
"Greek head on right Yankee shoulders." [15] She
opposed an outmoded and therefore time-
consuming plainness of dress; in this case, it was
easiest and best to follow custom. She saw little
point in freighting her letters with repetitions of
good will among relatives; the affection was real
and needed no constant restatement. When
Waldo asked "Are not the affections in our own

power?" she had the sense to say "No!" In fact, this and the following reply to Waldo suggest that she was the more abandoned in love—and in love, it is reasoned abandon that deserves the respect of common sense.

I've more independence than to be governed by the measure my friend deals to me—if he merits love I'm sure I care not if he gives me but a pint [;] I shall give him an ocean [,] and have confidence that as far as I merit I also shall receive—and although you may say—if you wish to be loved [,] love—I say—you may not always be loved in proportion as you love.[16]

Her affection for nature showed itself partly in a quantity of pets: a lamb, a canary, white mice, squirrels, a spaniel, her riding horse. She also enjoyed whatever New Concord provided of violets, golden rod, moonlight, and "trees in the glory of full blossom—without one single leaf of green." Again,

Oh what glorious sunsets we have [.] I recollect when I was a *very* little girl that I never was so much angered or disturbed by anything that a dawn of glory or an eve of beauty like unto this could not insensibly calm the tumult.[17]

Indeed, it may well be that Ellen's intense love of the out-of-doors was made so vivid to Waldo by his love of her, that for the first time in his life he experienced something more than a bookish and theoretical appreciation of nature.[18]

- 2 -

ELLEN'S KNOWLEDGE of books included, as we have seen, the Bible, and at one time she had read

Dr. Doddridge "a good deal." Her marked copy
of *Sabbath Recreations; or, Select Poetry of a
Religious Kind,* still exists.[19] In spite of Aunt
Mary's hope that she did not speak French, Ellen
did, and Waldo used it when writing of love in her
album and when speaking of love in a grove north
of Concord.[20] She knew little or no Shakespeare,
but some Herbert, Thomson, Young, Campbell,
Scott, Southey, and Byron—as well as the works
of a number of minor lady poets.[21] She quoted
Bryant, mentioned gift books and other anthologies, and was at least acquainted with *Pilgrim's
Progress.*[22] Waldo influenced her to read Robert-
son's *Charles V* and perhaps Channing's "Inaugu-
ral discourse." [23]

And Ellen had opinions about her reading.
Waldo wrote that she knew "the difference between good poetry & bad." Bryant's "Death of
the Flowers" was "meat & drink" to her.[24] She
would not call Scougal's *Life of God in the Soul
of Man* morose, but she believed that "what he
thinks loses some of its weight by repetition in
different words." Compared with Scougal, Ir-
ving's *History of Columbus* and *Conquest of Gra-
nada* were "jellies." Scott's *Anne of Geierstein*
interested her, but she would not judge it until she
reached the end. Everyone she knew liked Cather-
ine Maria Sedgwick's *Clarence,* but Ellen could
not: "the characters in general are like all in novels—saving the heroine who is as perfectly unat-
ural [*sic*] as a spirit." Occasional exuberances of
her own style she derided with parenthetical remarks such as "Oh the metaphorical droppings of

a girl in her teens," and "booh!! booh!! what a figuration and how finished." She commented intelligently on other arts also: on Benjamin West's "Christ Rejected," and on music. In one letter she told Waldo

The desire that it *creates* Good musick *satisfies* and is not wholesome food for the soul that revels in it as *I* do—It says "seek no farther" [;] it deadens all longings for any thing better than itself—this is the character of a great part of beautiful musick [,] though I own sometimes the soul by the stirring sentiment of the songs and a tune well adapted may be excited to nobler hopes & wishes—And it is (strange as it may appear) more apt to have this effect upon an auditor than a performer.[25]

Ellen had literary ambitions of her own and wrote verses. Her muse was often, as she called it during her engagement, "a disobedient lady," but she hoped to write more after marriage. Illness was, as we would expect, a great frustrator of her work.

God has given me a harp, and the strings I believe are sound and sweet but the part which holds them [—] the bridge [,] the fretts [—] are weak and wasting—Every day I ought to get one drop from my brain of clear distilled essence—I ought—but ah!![26]

Another difficulty was occasional weakness within her own character—for example, failure to keep a resolution: "I am astonished how it injures the harmony of the harp—it will jar now for long days."[27]

Like most persons in love, she confessed that

her letters could not express the intensity of her
affection; often they were, however, felicitous in
style and enlivened by effective metaphors.[28]
Charming in their spontaneity, wit, and variety,
they are, indeed, better in their genre than her
poetry.

Waldo thought at the time of their engagement
that Ellen made "fine verses," and later remembered that they were "as easy as breathing to her
who wrote." [29] To the modern reader, most of her
serious verse (chiefly in conventional quatrains)
seems sentimental, excessively trite in rhythm and
rhyme and imagery, sometimes badly mixed in met-
aphor. Yet its sounds are often pleasant, and if
she left no excellent poems she at least left some
attractive lines.

> . . . *When winter reigned I'd close my eye, but wake*
> *with bursting spring*
> *And live with living Nature, a pure rejoicing thing.*
>
> *And Hope, sweet bird & kind, at last has flown*
> *And of her beauty scarce a trace is found*
> *Save . . . there a golden feather quivering on the ground—*
> *Just bright enough to cheat the eager eye*
> *Just strong enough temptation for a lie.*[30]

Ellen had at least equal talent for humorous verse
(as in the rhyming journals), and one of her most
successful poems combines playfulness with a serious emotion.

> *Love scatters oil*
> *On Life's dark Sea*
> *Sweetens its toil*
> *Our helmsman he*

Around him hover
Odorous clouds
Under his cover
His arrows he shrouds.

The cloud was around me
I knew not why
Such sweetness crowned me
While Time shot by.

No pain was within
But calm delight
Like a world without sin
Or a day without night.

The shafts of the god
Were tipped with down
For they drew no blood
And knit no frown.

I knew not of them
Till Cupid laughed loud
And saying "You're caught!"
Flew off in the cloud.

Oh then I awoke
And I lived but to sigh
I've done with grief now
I shan't tell why.[31]

Her achievement was slight, but her verses may have been, as Waldo later thought, "on the way to all high merits." [32]

With her intelligence and her interest in writing, Ellen offered Waldo companionship of the mind which well supported and supplemented their emotional affinities. Her letters by no means

had the erudition or profundity of the Emerson-
Carlyle correspondence; but her letters did have
some intellectual content, and that content as well
as everything else about her mind must have been
highly congenial to Waldo.

- *3* -

INEVITABLY, ALL Ellen's affection and virtue, her
spirituality, intelligence, and art were affected by
her consumption. "Sell my wealth for a healthy
winter—yes willingly" she wrote, and the possibility of an early death lurked in the background of
letters and poems.[33] It is not remarkable that she
was depressed from time to time: "What is this
unaccountable feeling weeping and for what?" [34]
But it is remarkable that so often she faced present suffering and bitter prospects with vitality
and gaiety. She hated to burden others with her
black moods; she looked "with faith for sunnier
hours—these are not *dark*—but a little paly." [35] In
Waldo's words, "the moment the queen of me
gets relief from one of her ill turns her spirits
return also & she is . . . social as ever tho' her
sociability is imprisoned in whispers." [36]

Some of her courage came from Waldo's love
and careful nursing, some from her mother's "pattern of patience." [37] The exercise that was strongly
recommended by Waldo and others gave her not
only hope of recovery, but also frequent evidence
of it. Immediately after her engagement she resolved on skating lessons, and probably took

them. She had had riding lessons in Boston, and rode as well as walked a great deal in and around New Concord.[38] Carriage drives were helpful, as were the two long trips with Waldo.[39] After all, Waldo's strength was slowly gaining and Mr. Ware was at least holding his own. Why might not Ellen do as well? And there was always the consoling belief that even if she and Waldo should have but a brief union on earth, they would have an eternal one hereafter. Ellen's faith in immortality and reunion was explicit and strong.[40]

Her courage was sustained, finally, by her sense of humor. Waldo tells of her playfulness, of their calling her troubles "red wheezers." [41] Her letters delight in Scotch dialect, and in nicknames: Doctor Jackson was "Betty Jackson"; Waldo was not only the King but "Grampa"—so many years her senior; she herself was necessarily the Queen, ironically "Grandma," and schizophrenically both "Lady Penseroso" and "Lady Frolick." Lady Frolick dominated her letters—sometimes to a degree that Ellen thought she should be ashamed of: "Are you not tired [of my facetiousness]? and will you love me always in spite of all my nonsense and folly?" [42]

She called herself "a weak butter tub" and ridiculed long Tucker noses—as well as Waldo's. "I love you very much," she told him, then added "I would like to have you love me always if consistent with your future plans." [43] She made humor of their visit to the Canterbury Shakers, whose Sister Winkley gave them "a long & earnest sermon on the 'beauty of virginity.' " [44] To the rhyming journal of a trip they made after marriage, she contributed this quatrain.

> *A dear little mouse not owning a house*
> *And feeling my boot was a cold one*
> *To my sole applied friction. 'Tis past contradiction*
> *The act was a marvellous bold one.*[45]

Very little was immune from her wit: of Waldo in Philadelphia during the same trip, "not a text has he expounded [,] not a skeleton of a sarmint has he formed [,] not a sonnet has he perpetrated"; of her first housekeeping "no cake—bless me how many eggs? how much sugar? . . . only imagine the careless, one eyed sluttish Ellen Tucker in this situation." [46] She gibed at her own verse and occasional flights of elevated prose. Best of all is the sauciness of these lines addressed to the young Reverend Mr. Emerson:

> *When we're angels in heaven*
> *Dont raving mad be*
> *If without notice given*
> *I stay out to tea. . . .*
>
> *I shan't keep a carriage*
> *My wings will be strong*
> *And our earthly marriage*
> *Will be vain as a song.*
>
> *I therefore shall use them*
> *As I may see fit*
> *And tea out and dine out*
> *Nor mind you a bit.*[47]

- *4* -

ELLEN'S IS not, of course, the only character revealed by her relations with Waldo. He appears

too, multifaceted, occasionally depressed, often
happy, sometimes gayer and less reserved than in
any other of his seventy-nine years.

Some of his comments about love were as trite
as other men's; his love poems were not greatly
better than hers; and when he stole a note written
about him by Ellen, or made her his "Ellinelli,"
his "Queen," he was obviously not yet Holmes's
priest from Concord Delphi.[48] Nowhere else did
he write as he did in one of her albums
" 'L'Amitié est l'Amour sans ailes,' et mon affection, ma belle reine, est une Amitié amoureuse,
puisqu'elle a tout le feu de l'amour, mais elle n'a
point d'ailes; pas une plume. Oh Ellen, elle ne
peut pas mouvoir; c'est un rocher." [49] He had
shown a sense of humor well before he met her,
but her gaiety stimulated an increased response
from him. Flashes of humor occur in his verse;
the rhymed chronicle "Meredith Village" shows
him at his most effervescent—readiest to enjoy
travel, nonsense, and human rather than bookish
company.[50] Further humor enlivens at this time his
correspondence with others, but probably the best
is lost with his letters to her—letters she called
"instructive & amusing—merry yet solid." [51] Once
she had to scold him for what he said in a letter,
but most of her difficulties were in curbing his
impatience to see her. He asked her to say that
she loved him, and reported how he had praised
her to William.[52] Before they were married he
may have sent her some of his journals to read;
certainly he was anxious to read hers. He shared

with her the latest news of his brothers' health, the honor of his being chosen Chaplain of the State Senate, and the sensations of revisiting one of his early homes near Boston. He asked her to contribute to a charity; she responded with twenty dollars. She knew that he sensed the dignity of his new pastorate, and that he did not "love musick extravagantly" though he wrote as though he *"felt"* it.[53]

Stephen Whicher has written that "no relationship, not even the beautiful dream of his first marriage, ever meant as much to . . . [Emerson] as that with his brothers . . . —above all, Charles." [54] Yet Charles himself, who was at the young couple's home "often, in & out," complained to Edward and William that

Waldo is so busy . . . I see little of him. I wonder if everybody is lost to their brothers & all ties of blood & sympathy, the moment they are settled & married? I suppose I quarrel with what is a necessary state of things. . . . I mean not to murmur at any neglect—not a bit—I mean just what I say—to wonder whether t'is [sic] the invariable effect of business & marriage to make one independent of, & therefore indifferent to old relationships & intimacies.[55]

In fact, all the evidence supports the opinion of Ralph L. Rusk—author of the authoritative life of Emerson, and chief editor of Emerson's letters—that Ellen stirred Waldo "more than anybody else ever had done or could do." [56] It was Henry James's opinion that "certain chords in Emerson . . . did not vibrate at all," and many

critics have agreed one such chord was that of
"outgoing affection and compassion which we
rightly value in other authors." [57] We can understand such an opinion from anyone who has
known only the older Emerson or the public
Emerson, but we must correct it because of what
is now known about his response to Ellen. That
response illustrates, and perhaps prompted, these
lines in his "Initial, Daemonic, and Celestial
Love."

> *The maid, abolishing the past,*
> *With lotus wine obliterates*
> *Dear memory's stone-incarved traits,*
> *And, by herself, supplants alone*
> *Friends year by year more inly known.*
> *When her calm eyes opened bright,*
> *All else grew foreign in their light.*
> *It was ever the self-same tale,*
> *The first experience will not fail;*
> *Only two in the garden walked,*
> *And with snake and seraph talked.*[58]

If Waldo intellectualized his love for Ellen, as
has been charged [59] and as is no doubt partly true,
the intellectualizing occurred chiefly after her
death; the warmth and directness of his affection
while Ellen lived are clear from his poems and
journals of that time, and from correspondence.
"Oh Ellen, I do dearly love you—" burst out
among journal entries of religion and history.[60]
"Never again" was he "to write verse of such
singing sweetness as in the lyrics inspired by
Ellen"; they "gave the lie to the legend of emotional poverty he had been trying to attach to

himself." [61] The love poems he finished while they
were together totaled about a dozen. They are
conventional in rhetoric and form, yet their unre-
served affection is a bright part of this halcyon
period. One of the best is "Thine Eyes Still
Shined."

> *Thine eyes still shined for me, though far*
>   *I lonely roved the land or sea:*
> *As I behold yon evening star,*
>   *Which yet beholds not me.*
>
> *This morn I climbed the misty hill*
>   *And roamed the pastures through;*
> *How danced thy form before my path*
>   *Amidst the deep-eyed dew!*
>
> *When the redbird spread his sable wing,*
>   *And showed his side of flame;*
> *When the rosebud ripened to the rose,*
>   *In both I read thy name.*[62]

THREE

Winged for Flight

"There is a kind of contempt of the landscape felt by him who has just lost by death a dear friend. The sky is less grand as it shuts down over less worth in the population."

Nature, *end of chapter 1.*

THE FOREGOING portraits of Queen and King have been drawn chiefly from the period of their engagement, but have borrowed some details from the period of marriage—marriage that began, as has been said, on September 30, 1829.

The honeymoon trip—if any—was brief, for the newlyweds expected to reach their new home on the fifth of October.[1] They had chosen Mrs. Keating's boardinghouse in Chardon Street, Boston, and before the end of the month Waldo reported them "very pleasantly situated." Ellen's wish about her family was fulfilled, for her sisters Margaret and Paulina with Mr. and Mrs. Kent were boarding in the same house.[2]

Ellen's income from her father's estate quickly

made a difference in Waldo's way of life. Each of
them had his own "equipage"—at a time when
only one other family in the congregation went to
church in a carriage.³ They subscribed to *The
New Jerusalem Magazine, Christian Examiner,
North American Review,* and *Edinburgh Review.*⁴ Although Waldo worried some about his
expenses, he was willing to send $3.00 a week to
Edward, and, later, to help pay for Charles' study
of law.⁵

Charles saw that Ellen and Waldo were a "pair
imparadised," and he did not escape a wish by
Aunt Mary that "some gifted Ellen" would aid
his own development.⁶ (Waldo had already made
the same wish for William.) Ellen seemed very
well, and the only limit to their joy was Waldo's
rheumatic knee, so painful that he was unable to
walk without a cane, and had to sit while preach-
ing.⁷ Exercise had been enjoined on Ellen, so she
often walked, and every day the weather permitted she and Waldo rode.⁸ She wondered whether
"the Spirits in heaven look onward to their immortality as we on earth, or are absorbed in the
present moment"; ⁹ Waldo was interested in the
question, but also in nearer matters.

> And Ellen, when the graybeard years
>   Have brought us to life's evening hour,
> And all the crowded Past appears
>   A tiny scene of sun and shower,
>
> Then, if I read the page aright
>   Where Hope, the soothsayer, reads our lot,

Thyself shalt own the page was bright,
  Well that we loved, woe had we not,

When Mirth is dumb and Flattery's fled,
  And mute thy music's dearest tone,
When all but Love itself is dead
  And all but deathless Reason gone.[10]

- 2 -

THEIR FIRST separation occurred in November
when Waldo went to New Concord for two days
to give a reading and offer a prayer at the dedica-
tion of the new Unitarian church.[11] In the Spring
came a longer trip and a longer separation; Ellen's health had declined, and two months of Philadelphia's milder climate might help her.

She, Waldo, and Margaret left Boston about
the eighth of March, and with several overnight
stops traveled through Framingham, Worcester,
and Springfield to Hartford. On Saturday, Waldo
fetched Aunt Mary from Weathersfield for her
first meeting with Ellen [12]—a meeting which must
have been much anticipated on both sides. They
had been corresponding for more than a year, and
Aunt Mary—who enjoyed a formidable reputation for blunt speech—had already chided Ellen
for "the intimation you wanted more variety or
was not accustomed [*sic*] to have two days
alike." [13] Ellen, for her part, well knew her husband's high regard for this eccentric and electric
spinster. Here was Ellen's most difficult test in
meeting her new family.

Ellen's praise of Aunt Mary immediately after the meeting was enthusiastic, yet so expressed that it almost constituted a self-description.

> *She will dwell upon our mind,*
> *Flesh and blood so well refined*
> *That one questions whether death,*
> *Wasted form, or loss of breath*
> *Will be in her path to heaven,—*
> *All her body seems to glow*
> *With her spirit's action so.*[14]

Concerning her own success with this paragon, Ellen was slyly modest.

> *Aunt Mary's eyes her niece did scan*
> *Compared it with her previous plan,*
> *The building was not half so fine . . .*
> *But hard enough to like she tries*
> *To faults determined closed her eyes*
> *And wouldn't mind them.*[15]

Blunt Aunt Mary may well have told Ellen the nature of her success, for the first of these verses are very close to the report Aunt Mary immediately sent to Edward: "I like her better better than I dreamt—but not near so handsome—genius and loveliness are enough." [16] To Waldo Aunt Mary extolled Ellen's "simple unsophisticated mode." [17]

In Hartford Waldo preached three times on Sunday, and on the next day they covered the thirty-four miles to New Haven in eight hours. Ellen's health was disappointing, but she was able to walk out of doors three times on Tuesday. Both Wednesday and Thursday were taken up with the trip on Long Island Sound to New York. "We got on board the boat at 6 A.M." Waldo wrote,

& expected to be at N. Y. at 4 P.M. But a gale came up from the Southwest which we cd. not weather & so at 12 o'clock we made into Norwalk roads as well as we could & came to anchor. There we lay panting & snuffing the insufferable mephitis of the cabin, & hearing the rain patter & looking at each other grimly, forty stout passengers, (though fortunately only two beside E. & M. in the ladies cabin) & lastly sleeping or trying to sleep in an air that wd doubtless have put out a lamp on the floor. But morning came, the wind abated, & the steam chimney began once more to puff. The clouds broke, & we were repaid for our troubles by a noble passage up the Sound— fine sun [,] mild air, swift vessels, beautiful shores, noble seats—& through all—got to this long London town—to the American Hotel at 2 o'clock. . . . You may imagine I bit my lips with mortification to find I had got the queen into this bad navigable box. She bore it very well—all but the impossibility of sleep.[18]

Ellen's own description of the adventure is more gay than wry.

> *Who that had good feet*
> *Who that owned a shilling*
> *In a stage to get a seat*
> *To be soaked in a boat is willing?* . . .
> *O the delight of spending a night*
> *On board of a steam packet*
> *Down below, grovelling woe,*
> *Above, cold rain and racket.*[19]

Though the strain had left her "quite weak," she insisted that they stay in New York only two nights;[20] so on Saturday by way of the Raritan River, they went on to the

Fair land of bonnets white and neat
Of taste so pure   of streets so clean
That here the first pigs we have seen. . . .
Thy spotless fame will melt away
Beware   Oh Philadelphia!!! [21]

They stopped at a hotel, but Waldo's friends helped them quickly secure room and board with Miss McElroy at Eleventh and Chestnut Streets [22] –good lodgings though one morning

A little insect rich & red
With our own hearts blood on the blanket played.

Fortunately

A well spread table does the dame display
Neat though not rare & splendid —in its way.[23]

Waldo helped Ellen and Margaret get settled, preached three sermons, visited the waterworks and pagoda, and enjoyed his childhood friend, William H. Furness.[24] Furness lived near the boardinghouse, and described Ellen as "a delicate little creature." Once he found her and Waldo "walking with arms around each other, up & down their parlor. He borrowed my Humes' Hist of England [.] Reluctant to inflict dry reading upon his child-wife, he said he would have her begin with the reign of Queen Eliz.th" [25]

Waldo was concerned that at Miss McElroy's there were no women in the family except the hostess, and that Ellen was not sufficiently robust, so he lingered. Yet to Aunt Mary he confessed he was

getting to be sadly impatient of my life here, which has petty engagements which tear time into slivers, and are singularly unfavorable to any thing like intellectual progress. Oh fie that we—no—that I should be so enthralled to small accidents, that the first derangement of my domestic routine should put a chain on the wheels of the spirit—& the old trains of thot are broken up—the landmarks are gone—the favorite speculations grow faint & dim, and when I come back to my arm chair, I shall be recreated not enriched.[26]

Ellen knew his mood, and protested to Charles, "I have given him leave [,] yea have urged his going away *now*—for he is every whit as much out of his element as at *Concord N. H.*" [27] Finally, after about ten days in Philadelphia, he left for Boston, relieved that Ellen was "ramparted round with troops of friends. She seems better, & there is a good physician, and *there is a good Physician.*" [28]

They were not together again for a month and a half. Ellen and Margaret looked at some paintings but were much in the open air, interested in people, buildings, and nature; Mrs. Kent and Paulina came south for a visit.[29] Of Waldo's moods there is more evidence. He began "sonneteering" in March, and April was perhaps the month of "Thine Eyes Still Shined," [30] certainly of "To Ellen at the South."

> *The green grass is bowing,*
> *The morning wind is in it;*
> *'T is a tune worth thy knowing,*
> *Though it change every minute.*

'T is a tune of the Spring;
  Every year plays it over
To the robin on the wing,
  And to the pausing lover.

O'er ten thousand, thousand acres,
  Goes light the nimble zephyr;
The Flowers—tiny sect of Shakers—
  Worship him ever.

Hark to the winning sound!
  They summon thee, dearest,—
Saying, 'We have dressed for thee the ground,
  Nor yet thou appearest.

'O hasten; 't is our time
  Ere yet the red Summer
Scorch our delicate prime,
  Loved of bee,—the tawny hummer.

'O pride of thy race!
  Sad, in sooth, it were to ours,
If our brief tribe must miss thy face,
  We poor New England flowers. . . .

'Thou shalt command us all,—
  April's cowslip, summer's clover,
To the gentian in the fall,
  Blue-eyed pet of blue-eyed lover.

'O come, then, quickly come!
  We are budding, we are blowing;
And the wind that we perfume
  Sings a tune that's worth the knowing.' [31]

Finally plans were made for Waldo's going to
Philadelphia in mid-May, and by May 27 Ellen
and he were back in Massachusetts, settled with
his mother in a boardinghouse of Brookline. They

had a parlor and three chambers—one for the older Mrs. Emerson, one for Ellen and Waldo, one for guests—and looked forward to setting up, the three of them, their own household in the fall.[32] Charles visited frequently; he thought the house "an ugly oldfashioned pleasant comfortable place," Ellen "beautifuller than ever," and his mother happy in a "peaceful hermitage." [33]

- *3* -

UNFORTUNATELY CHARLES had soon to communicate bad news and well-founded fears. On August 11 he sent word to William and Edward that

Ellen was this morning attacked again by her old & deadly enemy the bleeding. It was a slight attack & she is now pretty comfortable, yet it is discouraging, it is so much ground lost. It casts trouble & anxiety over her husband's prospects.

Three days later,

Ellen is a little better. But we are in the depths & I may say mire of Doctors, Nurses, physic, & watching. . . . We hourly expect Mrs. Kent.[34]

On August 23 Edward arrived; he and Charles, both of them affectionate and clever, must have helped Ellen's spirits. Her mother took a room nearby. Soon Ellen felt so much better that she decided to travel.[35] Early in September Waldo accompanied her as far as Lexington, whence she continued to New Concord.[36] After two weeks Waldo joined her and preached in that Concord for the last time.[37]

Ellen's mending fast and bearing this slight trip must have influenced the decision on the more important question of whether to face another winter in the North. The whole family studied the pros and cons. Immediately after the attack of August 11, Charles had speculated that Ellen and Waldo would probably go south in the fall. As earlier, his were the most pessimistic of the family's letters, and he soon wrote that

Waldo feels the disappointment strongly, & seems now to make up his mind, that he must break or untie all bands that fasten him here, & go off in search of kinder elements. For my part, I doubt whether there is any climate that will save Ellen from the return of these attacks, & if there be such an one, she must live, not visit there.

A month later, Charles apparently believed the couple should not go away.[38] Aunt Mary inclined towards their going; Ellen, towards staying home. She and Waldo "ponder[ed] many plans." [39]

The crucial voice was that of Doctor Jackson. By late August he was discouraging a voyage; [40] in late September he expressed "a decided opinion that it was needless to go away, [better] to spend the winter quietly keeping house like good & sensible people." [41] Ellen should not "migrate to Cuba or elsewhere unless she was prepared to stay for ten years." [42] Any of several hypotheses may have caused his decision: that Ellen really could survive a Boston winter, that she was too weak to travel far, or that she was doomed in any case and might die happier if close to familiar places and persons.

Ellen and Waldo probably accepted the advice because of Doctor Jackson's reputation, but there were also the known hazards of travel at sea, Waldo's professional responsibilities, and the pleasure of anticipating for the first time their own home.

With the decision against travel firmly made, Ellen and Waldo began to buy carpet and other furnishings; by mid-October they were living on Chardon Street again, in the house that had been Mrs. Keating's but was now their own.[43] Waldo's mother was with them and happy to have "just that degree of care" that she wanted.[44] Ellen was

happier than it often falleth to the lot of mortals to be. . . . Here I sit in my own little domicile & *realize* that I am Mrs Emerson to the full for [the servants] Betsy & Nancy and Martin must have their daily & nightly tasks allotted—and Mr Such a one with his wife are in town and they must come to tea tomorrow.[45]

Her Thanksgiving guests included Charles, the Tuckers, the Farnhams, and some aunts who lived on Boylston Street.[46] A week later, "grandfather" Ripley visited for several days and preached for his grandson.[47] Aunt Mary appeared briefly.[48]

The impression is of a household far too active for Ellen's health: both her and Waldo's families were large and closely knit, each group got along well with the other, and apparently everyone enjoyed family visits. Ellen may have strained herself in playing hostess; yet she had servants, and the record of her responsibilities comes from letters and a journal—much more likely to record the visits breaking a household routine than to detail the quiet days of routine itself.

Meanwhile, all was not well with Waldo's brothers. Charles still felt cut off from him.

I live in solitude nearly as entire as if I were in the woods. . . . The reward I look forward to all the week, is my talk with Waldo on Saturday. I love him; altho' his own affections seem all called in & centred on Ellen.

Apparently as an afterthought and to soften the charge, he added, above *affections*, "except a universal benevolence." [49] He used to come to Chardon Street "with the juvenile elegance of leisure, & the provincial appetite for conversation" only to find his brother surrounded by "press of cares & a plethory [*sic*] of talk and excitement." [50]

Edward's trouble was greater. He had been taken ill in New York—and with symptoms like Ellen's. There was debate whether he should stay in New York, where William could look after him, or go to Boston, Florida, or the West Indies; in December he sailed for St. Croix.[51]

By then Ellen was less well herself, and in spite of their new home and the decision that had been made to stay in Boston, both she and Waldo were longing for a milder climate. Their hopes and obligations warred against the facts and prognosis of her health. To Edward she sent a special request.

Pray . . . pick out a pretty spot for Waldo & wife to live—for such golden dreams in spite of 2d church and blk gown Bostonians & Concordians do I indulge. . . . Cold

winds and changes here [,] scorpions & debilities there —
The latter I urge are not so soul annoying as the former —
One is a slow, uncertain death or an ill-spent life [,] the
other a quick and sure remedy or a certain an [*sic*] not
agreeable but more preferable death — You perhaps are so
new to & transient in the invalid table that you will never
understand me when I speak so strongly.[52]

Waldo seconded her request: "Pray make *written minutes* of places & prices & persons & climate
that may be of use to any of us hereafter." [53] An
extensive journal entry on the fear of death devel-
oped his thought that "the more delicate the struc-
ture of the mind the stronger this emotion." [54] In
late December the cold storms were very trying to
Ellen, but she went out in the air daily.[55]

- *4* -

FOR THE first month of the new year, 1831, Waldo's "Preaching Record" shows normal activity —
usually two sermons each Sunday. He did not
preach at all on February 6 and 13. The record
of sermons composed is more clearly ominous: six
for January, then none until "Consolation for the
Mourner" was written to be delivered on February 20.[56]

Charles began the year by reporting the surface, "We are all well here." [57]

Early in January Mrs. Kent raised some blood
and looked pale and thin.

"A drop of vermeil should be the family coat of
arms," said Ellen, anxious about her mother, con-

fessedly "very unwell" herself, surrounded by
pills, hoping to go to Philadelphia in six weeks.[58]

On the twelfth of January Waldo asked his
congregation, "How shall you more gratefully
awaken your heart and your conscience amid the
present despondency than by reflexions on . . .
that web of relations to all beings into which your
own lot is woven?" And he returned to the fear of
death, saying it "is unworthy of a man." [59]

The next day Ellen had another attack of
bleeding at the lungs. "At first it seemed as slight
as the last ill turn . . . , but her cough increased,
& other complaints. . . . The air was so reviving
to her that notwithstanding the wintry cold she
continued to ride almost every day." [60] Snow was
so severe that Waldo's morning service on January 16 was cancelled, and late in the month there
were higher snowbanks than Boston had known
for many years.[61] Waldo believed that if Ellen
could continue her brief rides he could "hope the
reestablishment of her health but we have come to
the prefixing of *if* to all our plans." [62] Doctor Jackson came daily. Her mother-in-law described
Ellen as "calm & patient under much suffering.
. . . The more she is known the better she is
loved. . . . Waldo bears with his usual firmness
his afflictions, . . . & by his unremitted efforts for
her comfort, aleivates [*sic*] her sufferings." [63]
There were rallies and relapses; [64] nurses rubbed
her hands to quicken her circulation; [65] Waldo,
Charles, and Mrs. Emerson sent frequent bulle-
tins to the family.

On the second of February, a Wednesday, she rode twice; Charles thought she was in no immediate danger, and Waldo felt encouraged. But when Charles returned on the fifth, he "found her sadly altered & her husband & mother without any hope of her recovery." She talked calmly about her death,[66] and "was humble & prayerful, frequently offering her petitions in short ejaculations . . . in her intervals from suffering—& expressing her gratitude to God, & her benevolent interest in all her friends, saying they *all* had been *very kind* to her." [67] She hoped she would live "to hear of Edward's safe arrival" in St. Croix.[68] Margaret as well as Mrs. Kent had arrived, and both were present during the last few days and nights.[69]

Early on Sunday, Charles thought Ellen might not survive the day; every breath was painful, and Waldo was "as one over whom the waters have gone." [70] Doctor Follen preached for Waldo in the morning; Mr. Frothingham in the afternoon.[71] At evening, Ellen was still alive, but her spirit seemed "winged for its flight." Charles wrote to Aunt Mary that

today (with the exception of perhaps two or three times a half hour) she has been in less pain—sometimes torpid under the influence of her opiates, but at others serene & fully conscious. She spoke this afternoon very sweetly of her readiness to die, that she told you she should not probably live through the winter, tho' she did not know that she should have been called so soon. She saw no reason why her friends should be distressed—it was better she should go first, & prepare the way. She asked Waldo if he had strength, to read her a few verses of scripture, and he read a portion of the XIV chapter of John [—possibly the verses beginning "In my Father's house are many mansions"]. Waldo is bowed down under the affliction. Yet he says tis like seeing an angel go to heaven.[72]

Her pain continued to be less severe that night. On Monday, Grandfather Ripley came, and Ellen said his prayer "was very 'refreshing' to her." Charles said his last good-by; Ellen told him

to cheer up Waldo when she was gone, not to let him think too much of her. 'He has his God as I have.' I was very thankful for the priviledge [sic] of thus taking leave of her. She looks saint like. I wish you could see & hear her for a moment. The House of mourning for such sufferers, is better than the House of feasting.[73]

Frequently she asked that Waldo be with her when she died, and he was; the record of her last hours is his.

A little after 2 o'clock on Tuesday morn, she said she felt that she was going soon & having asked if Mother, Margaret, & Paulina were all present she wished them to be still & she would pray with them. And truly & sweetly did she pray for herself & for us & infused such comfort into my soul as never entered it before & I trust will never escape out of it. After this she kissed all, & bid her nurses, 'love God;' & then sunk very fast, occasionally recovering her wandering mind. One of the last things she said after much rambling & inarticulate expression was 'I have not forgot the peace & joy.' And at nine o'clock she died.[74]

It was February 8, 1831. She had not lived to be twenty.

Henry Ware preached the funeral sermon;[75] and, in accordance with her own request, Ellen was buried in her father's tomb at Roxbury.[76]

FOUR

Years of the Widower

"The man or woman who would have remained a sunny gardenflower, with no room for its roots and too much sunshine for its head, by the falling of the walls and the neglect of the gardener is made the banian of the forest."

The last sentence of "Compensation"

EMERSON had been struck by an experience traditionally the most pathetic in human experience—the slow, painful, and early death of a beautiful, beloved wife. The depth and sorrow of his reaction were no exception to tradition; no other part of his life better shows the intensity as well as the characteristic complexity of his emotion. In a letter he wrote to Aunt Mary only two hours after Ellen's death some important elements of that complexity appear: grief anticipated but as yet overshadowed by release; an excitement of gratitude and admiration; the good of one person causing joy in another; faith in immortality.

My angel is gone to heaven this morning & I am alone in the world & strangely happy. Her lungs shall no more be

torn nor her head scalded by her blood nor her whole life
suffer from the warfare between the force & delicacy of
her soul & the weakness of her frame. I said this morn & I
do not know but it is true that I have never known a
person in the world in whose separate existence as a soul I
could so readily & fully believe & she is present with me
now beaming joyfully upon me, in her deliverance & the
entireness of her love. . . . I see it plainly that things &
duties will look coarse & vulgar enough to me when I find
the romance of her presence (& romance is a beggarly
word) withdrawn from them all. But now the fulness of
joy occasioned by things said by her in the last week & by
this eternal deliverance is in my heart.[1]

His mother recognized that the bereavement
was a much greater trial than any other he had
known, and reported that he bore the affliction
"with the patience, Fortitude, & humility, of a
christian." Not until mid-April could she see him
"better in spirits." [2]

During 1829 and 1830, everything in nature
had reminded him of love; now he read "his loss
in every utensil in his house, in every garment, in
the face of every friend." All his resources as a
writer expressed his grief: journal entries, quotations, verse, sermons, letters. On February 8,
1831, he recorded Ellen's death in a single sentence; when he resumed his journal five days later
it was to praise her and lament his own unworthi-
ness, to describe her death and a dream he had
had of her dying, to invoke her good influence, to
pray for relief from the "miserable debility" into
which he had sunk, but to recognize that no relief
could restore the rapture they had shared. He

quoted a Latin epitaph, "Alas! how much less pleasing is it to dwell with those who are left than to remember thee!" [3]

In verses scattered through his blotting books he said that if he lost faith in Ellen's remembering herself and him he would bury his ambition, regretted that she had not visited him in dreams yet implied that her love embraced him in other ways, and hoped that he would live well enough to join her in heaven.[4] None of these fragments was ever prepared by Emerson for publication; they remained private laments.

His responsibility to the Second Church called him, of course, to re-enter the pulpit as soon as possible. Twelve days after Ellen's death he resumed his preaching, using the new sermon "Consolation for the Mourner." To its editor this sermon showed "the young minister's concern not to obtrude his private affairs into the pulpit. . . . Yet he seeks to make his personal experience a bridge by which to cross over to the thoughts and emotions of his listeners." [5]

After having emphasized that *"it never occurs to* a mind at all enlarged by religion . . . *to murmur and repine"* when bereaved, or to feel malice towards the pleasures of those who do not mourn, Emerson expounds the ways in which Christianity removes fear of death from both the dying and the survivors. He stresses the desire a survivor will have to be reunited with his loved one through his own death, but points out that duty binds us to this life, and the dead will approve us only if we discharge our duties well. Such are his main ideas.

The tone of the full text and Emerson's known methods of composition argue that he could truthfully have written *"I* have not murmured or repined . . . ; *I* have not felt malice." And certain passages speak with unusual directness of his own memories.

The Christian faith teaches us that the soul does not die but is separated from the body and enters into a nearer relation to the Father of Spirits. . . . And the Christian soul, as it departs out of life, affirms it cheerfully to those who weep. . . .

In these our friends who are gone, we now seem to possess a *personal interest of love, of intercession in the spiritual society.* The soul that has thought with us, and preferred our interest to its own, and known well what was in our heart, is now only a step removed from us, and we believe, looks back with more than earthly love, mixing the recent knowledge of human wants, with the newness of the revelations now made to it by change of state. . . .

The only true and enduring bond that can unite souls is the love of the same excellence.

Finally, by feelings stimulated from the New Testament

and by the spectacle of triumphant faith the dying chamber of youth where a thousand expectations are shattered may infuse more sweetness and joy into the soul than ever prosperity or praise could give.[6]

Waldo's letters to Edward and William show that his life had lost much of its value while death had become attractive. As his friends and even the members of his household tended to forget Ellen, his loneliness became more acute. Much of his solace came—atypically for him—from retrospection.[7] He received a packet of Ellen's early letters to her mother and Margaret: "pleasant pleasant it is to me to fill up link by link the diamond chain of so lovely a history." [8]

He had foreseen that his apathy would wear off. Old duties would present themselves as no longer repulsive; "I shall go again among my friends with a tranquil countenance. Again I shall be amused, I shall stoop again to little hopes & little fears." [9] In March, according to his mother, he was performing his "usual duties though . . . with a heavy heart." [10] In April, according to his journal "the formal duties . . . to be formally discharged" surrounded him though without lessening his grief.[11] In June he was asked to be the Phi Beta Kappa poet at Harvard, but declined because he felt in the spirit for writing dirges only.[12] Late in the year he railed against routines: "I am imprisoned in the forms & uses of every day, & cannot surrender myself to the sweet bitterness of lamenting my beauty, my glory, the life of my life." [13]

One custom exempt from that complaint was his daily walk, in the early morning, to Ellen's grave—a custom he is reported to have continued in all weather until leaving for Europe late in 1832.[14] In "Consolation for the Mourner" he had wondered

how the grave was ever frightful to us. When we have explored our desolate house for what shall never there be

The front view of the Concord, New Hampshire house in which Ellen Tucker and Ralph Waldo Emerson were married. The house was then owned by Ellen's stepfather, Colonel William A. Kent. It has since been moved to a new site and is now owned by Mr. and Mrs. Robert Beyer.

ELLEN LOUISA TUCKER. *Courtesy of Concord Antiquarian Society, Concord, Massachusetts. This photograph is of an original miniature painted by Sarah Goodridge in 1829 and given to Lucy Ann Withington of Park Street, Boston, Massachusetts. Miss Withington's grand-daughter presented the picture to the Concord Antiquarian Society in 1936.*

RALPH WALDO EMERSON. *Courtesy of Ralph Waldo Emerson Memorial Association. From the miniature by Sarah Goodridge, probably painted in 1829 before Emerson's marriage to Ellen Tucker in September. According to Emerson family tradition, this picture is a good likeness of Ralph Waldo Emerson at about the age of 26.*

The front entrance hall of the house in Concord, New Hampshire, in which Ellen Tucker and Emerson were married.

The north parlor of the Concord, New Hampshire house. According to tradition, Ellen Tucker and Ralph Waldo Emerson married in this room.

Boston – 20 Jany. 1828
Carver Street.

My dear William,

I only write that I may
avail myself of the kindness of Mrs Barnard who
to-day offered to send a letter, & that I may say some-
...

Sunday – 48

Boston Feby. 6

Dear William –

far dear Ellen is
on the brink of the grave – Every breath
is distress – She may not live the day
through. She has failed very rapidly
the past week – & when I saw her yesterday,
I was convinced I as well as her poor
husband must soon take leave of
her forever. Waldo is as you
may believe a one over whom the
waters have gone – Mother is well.
When you hear from Edward
you will let us immediately know.
If you have opportunity write him the
sad sad tidings.
God be with you &
all o'us –
Chas.

*Letter from Edward B. Emerson to his brother, William,
January 20, 1829. [The 1828 date given in the letter is in-
correct. 1829, noted on the mailing surface, is confirmed by
internal evidence.] Another letter to William February 6,
1831, comments on Ellen's continually worsening illness.
Courtesy of Dr. Ethel Emerson Wortis, New York City.*

Boston Sunday Eveg. Feby 6

Dear William —

When I wrote you today, it was in great haste, thinking the letter might go off at 1 o'clock. We have none of us, I believe, been aware until within two or three days of Ellen's immediate danger. I saw her last Wednesday — she was able to ride twice that day — & Waldo felt encouraged. Saturday morng. I came into town & found her sadly altered & her husband & mother without any hope of her recovery — You can think, my dear brother, how sad a house we are — Last night was a tedious & distressed one — today has been a little easier. She speaks of her situation, of her death with serenity & sweetness. This is a comfort to Waldo — He is bowed down under his affliction, but he says 'it is like nothing, but an angel taking her flight to Heaven.' Dr. Follen preached for W. this morning & Mr. Frothingham this afternoon. I am sure you will join your prayer with those we have this day offered in public & at home. — — Monday A.M. Ellen passed a more comfortable night than the one before it — She grows gradually weaker — but whenever she is free from pain, she talks cheerfully & expresses her thanks for all the kindness of those about her.

A letter from Charles Emerson to his brother, William Emerson, the evening of February 6, 1831. Two days before Ellen's death there was little hope for her recovery, and Ralph Waldo Emerson, emotionally afflicted by the inevitable, did not preach on that February Sunday. Courtesy of Dr. Ethel Emerson Wortis, New York City.

Cambridge - March. 1.

My dear brother.

And fare well to thee Winter -
Thou hast nipped a bud that was very beautiful
in our eyes - thou hast blighted hopes that were very
dear to our hearts - thou hast killed affections which
no Earthly Spring can renovate. Fare well to thee
grim Season - thou hast power ~~over us~~ over us & outward
nature for a few returning periods of time - But rage
as thou wilt, thou canst not shun thy own dissolution.
~~~ The melting airs of Spring whisper thy dirge, &
the climbing Sun in the Ecliptic, kindles thy funeral pile. So to the good shall be the end of
life. A chilly state of being - of contracted powers,
interrupted growth, dreary decay, shall give place to
thought how boundless, to love how ardent, to
bliss how perfect!

You have my letter of a week
ago. William - but I have not yet your answer.
Yet I am afraid I know well enough what &.

We are having lovely weather - To day
I heard Peter O. Thatcher Esq. address the

---

*Letter from Charles Emerson to his brother, William Emer-
son, on March 1, 1831. Charles here laments Ellen's death of
February 8, 1831. The 'nipped bud' refers to the beloved
Ellen, who after suffering with consumption died when she
was only nineteen years old. Courtesy of Dr. Ethel Emerson
Wortis, New York, City.*

New York, June 12, 1831.

Dear Mother,

I suppose before this you must have seen Col. Kent & his family, whom I had the pleasure of seeing here a few days ago. Miss Margaret appears feeble, but in good spirits. On the whole I think all their friends will congratulate them on the result of their excursion. — Mr John Joy has just been here to inform me of the return of his mother & their party. He says they are all well. Mrs Joy was unfortunately exposed in one storm near Washington, & was made ill by it for a week, but according to John, is quite well now, except her cough. I hope to see them this evening. Last Sabbath evening I was gratified, with hundreds beside, by hearing Dr Channing discourse on the text "Honor all men". It was full of large & noble ideas, philosophical, humane, & practical; worthy of the maturity of his mind & of his fame.

I don't think of any thing else that is worth telling of, so good bye, says your aff son

A letter from William Emerson to his mother, Ruth Haskins Emerson, on June 12, 1831. Colonel and Mrs. Kent and their daughter, Margaret, had left for a trip to the West Indies in March, 1831, shortly after Ellen's death. Mrs. Kent and Margaret also suffered from consumption. Here William Emerson, who saw them in New York on their return trip in June, remarks that Margaret appeared feeble. Her health did not improve, and she died on November 24, 1832. Courtesy of Dr. Ethel Emerson Wortis, New York City.

seen, we return with an eagerness to the tomb as the only
place of healing and peace. It seems to us that willingly—
oh yes, joyfully, we would, if permitted, lay down our
head also on the same pillow.[15]

A little over a year later his journal shows the
isolated entry, presumably recording a dream, "I
visited Ellen's tomb & opened the coffin." [16]

In March of 1831, Waldo and Charles made a
longer sentimental journey—an afternoon's walk
to their former home in Canterbury. Waldo had
written to Ellen about a similar visit two years
earlier.[17] Now, wrote Charles, "it was very pleasant to W. yet he feels with that line in Wordsworth's Ode 'that wheresoever he goes'

A beauty & a loveliness have passed away from Earth.

He is pretty well—not very—he is debilitated—
unstrung—feels his 'nature within him weary of
itself.' " [18]

Soon after that trip Waldo proposed another,
westward to "the mountain shires"

> *where old woods,*
> *Not tamed and cleared, cumber the ground*
> *With their centennial wrecks. . . .*
> *There will I bring my books,—my household gods,*
> *The reliquaries of my dead saint, and dwell*
> *In the sweet odour of her memory.*[19]

Part of this wish was fulfilled through a fortnight's ramble with Charles through Vermont in
early June. If the trip was intended to soften sad
memories, it largely failed. Waldo put in his journal only one brief record of the sights he saw, but

several poems about death—Ellen's and his own.[20]
In one fragment, beginning

> *O pleasant pleasant in my eye*
> *The grave is become,*

the handwriting becomes irregular, finally illegible; then in prose he twice calls "dearest Ellen." The passage is unusual, probably unique, in his journals, as evidence of anguish at times uncontrollable.[21]

Back in Boston, Waldo wrote to William that his journey had been "a strange one so pleasant & cheering & yet so sad. My memory is a bitter sweet."[22] Yet four days earlier he had written a journal entry which was significant because, although it starts with Ellen, it subtly shifts to some of Waldo's more habitual concerns. It does not suggest that his loss was being intellectualized away, but that intellectual activity, like routine, was consuming more and more of the time recently given to conscious grief.

After a fortnight's wandering . . . yet finding you dear Ellen nowhere & yet everywhere [,] I come again to my own place, & would willingly transfer some of the pictures that the eyes saw, in living language to my page; yea translate the fair & magnificent symbols into their own sentiments. But this were to antedate knowledge. . . . Only in God's own order & by my concurrent effort can I get the abstract sense of which mountains, sunshine, thunder, night, birds, & flowers are the sublime alphabet.[23]

During the first half of 1832, problems related to his ministry increasingly demanded Emerson's attention, and no doubt helped to decrease his consciousness of grief. Those problems culminated in his resigning from the Second Church; then he was in Europe from December, 1832, to October, 1833. Through this trip he ultimately achieved as much recovery from Ellen's death as he was ever to know.

Having landed in Malta, by March he was in Naples, "lonely. . . . Though a hermit such as I, may find his profit now & then in going alone to these old places, yet the true way for profit & delight doubtless is, to come & see them with those whose society is our daily food." [24] The direction of his longing is even clearer in lines written also in Naples, and alluding to Ellen's poem "The Violet."

> *Not many men see beauty in the fogs*
> *Of close low pine-woods in a river town;*
> *Yet unto me not morn's magnificence . . .*
> *Nor wit, nor eloquence,—no, nor even the song*
> *Of any woman that is now alive,—*
> *Hath such a soul, such divine influence,*
> *Such resurrection of the happy past,*
> *As is to me when I behold the morn*
> *Ope in such low moist roadside, and beneath*
> *Peep the blue violets out of the black loam,*
> *Pathetic silent poets that sing to me*
> *Thine elegy, sweet singer, sainted wife.*[25]

Several months later, in England, he told Carlyle about Ellen.[26] He had many important experiences—meetings with Landor, Coleridge, and Wordsworth; museum visits that were crucial for

his understanding of art and science—yet those
lonely days in Naples remained vivid, and when,
eight years later, he wished in "Self-Reliance" to
show that "Travelling is a fool's paradise" he
went on to say that

Our first journeys discover to us the indifference of places.
At home I dream that at Naples, at Rome, I can be in-
toxicated with beauty and lose my sadness. I pack my
trunk, embrace my friends, embark on the sea and at last
wake up in Naples, and there beside me is the stern fact,
the sad self, unrelenting, identical, that I fled from.[27]

He brought Ellen's memory back from Europe,
but also stronger health and fresh sights which
stimulated old ambitions, dropping one gauze cur-
tain over the past while raising another from the
future. From this time on, Ellen's memory is much
less apparent in Emerson's letters, journals, and
works, but it never disappears. The next year is
not atypical. In May of 1834, he wrote "I am
born tranquil, . . . never a keen sufferer. I will
not affect to suffer." Yet three months earlier, on
the third anniversary of Ellen's burial, he had
written, "these last three years of my life are not
a chasm—I could almost wish they were—so brilliantly sometimes the vision of Ellen's beauty &
love & life come out of the darkness." [28]

- *2* -

THESE FIRST years without Ellen were not, of
course, filled simply with bitter memories, the
dullness of routine, and lonely travels. There were

meaningful personal contacts and important problems of finance, profession, and philosophy; all were affected by the breaking of "the diamond chain."

During the first two years after her death, Emerson's memory of Ellen was reinforced by frequent and affectionate contacts with Mrs. Kent and Margaret, and by the sad parallels between their lives and hers.

The trip south for health desired by Ellen and Waldo during the weeks before her death, was instead begun in March, 1831, by Mrs. Kent and Margaret. Waldo announced them to William in New York.

I send you my Mother & sister on their way southward— but two of the intended party dont go with them—one is in heaven, & the other walking in his little mill path—

But both Mrs. Kent & Margaret need the journey very much & I trust it will prove beneficial. They have been faithful faithful to Ellen, & if life is desirable *here* to them I pray they may find all of good & sweet it has.[29]

In June the ladies and Colonel Kent passed through New York on their return to Boston, and William wrote that "Miss Margaret appears feeble, but in good spirits. On the whole I think all their friends will congratulate them on the result of their excursion." [30] Waldo could agree only in part: Margaret did look least well, but neither seemed much strengthened.

During the summer the three apparently saw one another frequently, for Waldo said the women comforted him with kindness. Unfortu-

nately by August he had to write to Edward, still
in the West Indies, that

> my poor sister Margaret Tucker is now suffering in her
> turn from the deadly malady of her family. . . . I tell her
> & her mother that if they want to go to St. Croix this
> winter they must make a bargain with you to come to a
> Southern port, say Baltimore & escort them out, for
> Col. Kent will not risque himself upon the waters. . . .
> Sad sad it will be to me to lose my highminded sister &
> yet every star that sinks on this rises in the other firma-
> ment & makes the vision of that more full of glory &
> delight.[31]

Within three days Waldo rented a house for the
Kents in Central Court, Boston, and worked to
get it ready for them.[32] By September they lacked
"heart enough unsupported as they are to venture
to the South this winter. I fear a hard winter may
bereave me of them both. Whilst they live I keep
a living monument of Ellen. She will be farther
from my mortal sight when they are gone, & I
love them for themselves." But the women
showed improved health as the fall wore on.[33]

Meanwhile Ellen's other sister, Paulina, now
married to Joshua Nash of Boston, was in October "on the eve of being confined"; two months
later she had given birth to "a fine son." [34] Another link to Ellen came through Elizabeth
Tucker, a cousin who lived in Derry, New Hampshire and attended the Academy there. Emerson
was present at the Examination in November,
1831, apparently addressed the scholars, and had
"some sad some pleasant thoughts" while spend-
ing the day at Elizabeth's house. He promised her
a list of recommended books, and when he sent it

it repeated many of his recommendations to Ellen.[35]

In the next year, consumption was again fatal to a member of the Tucker family: on November 24, 1832, Margaret died. Both Charles [36] and Waldo tried to comfort her mother; in his journal Waldo bade Margaret

farewell . . . for a little time my kind & sympathizing sister. Go rejoice with Ellen . . . in God's free & glorious universe. Tell her if she needs to be told how dearly she is remembered [,] how dearly valued. . . . God comfort the bitter lonely hours which the sorrowing mother must spend here.

Farewell, dear girl . . . the only sister I ever had.[37]

In Malta, in February, Waldo composed an obituary for Margaret [38] not knowing Mrs. Kent was so ill that Mrs. Emerson wrote to Charles, "I regret that Waldo, is not likely to see her again, for he loves her much." [39] The fears were justified; a letter to Waldo in Florence told of Mrs. Kent's death. "Fast, fast," he wrote,

the bonds dissolve that I was so glad to wear. She has been a most kind & exemplary mother. . . . Does the heart in that world forget the heart that did beat with it in this? Do jealousies, do fears, does the observation of faults, intervene? Dearest friends, I would be loved by all of you: dearest friend! we shall meet again.[40]

- *3* -

SEVERAL MONTHS before Ellen and Waldo first met, he had mused on the insignificance of human life.

The sun will shine on your funeral as bright as he did at
your bridal day & for one word that is spoken of your
character ten twenty will be spoken of the settlement of
your estate.[41]

The proportion of one to ten may not have held in
Ellen's case, but lawyers did what they could to
reach it.

Soon after her death in 1831, Waldo thought
that if William and Edward could not help pay
the expenses of their feeble-minded brother Bulkeley, he (Waldo) would be able to handle them
"without difficulty, especially as it seems that
Ellen is to continue to benefit her husband whenever hereafter the estate shall be settled. . . . I
please myself that Ellen's work of mercy is not
done on earth, but she shall continue to help Edward & B. & Charles." [42]

William too needed help, but Waldo so far had
only hopes and could not make promises; even his
claim to Ellen's estate was uncertain; Mrs. Kent,
Margaret, and Paulina had legal interests in the
settlement, and Waldo did not want to offend
them by exercising all his own rights.[43] But in
January, 1832, John Hooker Ashmun, professor
of law at Harvard, took out letters of administration for Waldo and petitioned the Supreme Judi-
cial Court in Chancery for a writ directing Pliny
Cutler, Mrs. Kent "and the other surviving heirs,
to appear before the court 'to abide such order
and decree as to your Honors shall seem agreeable to equity and good conscience.' " [44]

Waldo was determined "to adhere to yᵉ right

remembering y^t there are worse things y^n being defrauded to wit, defrauding, though there is no occasion for using either of these words." He expected delays; what he did not expect was how his cooperating with part of the family to determine his rights would appear to the public and to Paulina and Joshua Nash.

Pestered was I sadly one day lately by a quoted conversation y^t came to my ear y^t ["] Mr. E. had refused all compromise with his wifes friends & was gone to law with them." For ye first time I saw to my sorrow y^t ye thing admitted of y^t face. The facts are y^t by a mutual advised consent we get ye Supreme Court to distribute ye estate, & I take no step without advising with Mr & Mrs Kent & Margaret Tucker; and if ever such a story shd. be quoted to you refer to those persons or to Mr Cutler. Capt. Nash very possibly takes another view of it but if he do, has certainly had opportunity to know better.[45]

Waldo and his brothers handled money amicably, but not he and his brother-in-law, Joshua Nash. Waldo's funds were before long exhausted in helping Charles, but still the Court gave no opinion.[46]

When Margaret died, her will left many legacies to "poor individuals connexions & friends, as also a free bed at the Hospital"; the income of an additional $15,000 went to Paulina, and Boston was given the refusal of the residual estate for a free high school for girls. In the opinion of Charles, the residual amount would not be large enough to establish the school, but would have been if a codicil had not left the $15,000 to Paulina. Obviously the Tucker sisters were well-to-do.[47]

Charles was a lawyer, so he became his brother's agent when Waldo left for Europe.[48] When Waldo returned he still had no inheritance, only plans for using it: he regretted that his family was scattered, and hoped Ellen's money would enable him "to buy a hearth somewhere to which we pious Æneases may return with our household gods from all the quarters of our dispersion." [49]

The continued litigation had not, of course, healed the breach between Waldo and the Nashes. Early in 1834 the Nashes were ill and in the south. Waldo wrote a long and friendly letter, recommending European travel, offering to help them in any way he could, and frankly acknowledging the breach. "Today," he said,

I have been reading verses & scraps of Ellen that only heighten my admiration & my sorrow every time I read them & I go to Aunt Washburn's to find some living thing that is related to her & I desire to assure her sister & her sisters husband of my warm good will to them. I grieve if there has been any cloud, but we have seen each other so little that perhaps sufficient opportunities of explanation have not occurred; but we ought to be so far bound to each other as the common love & reverence of the departed whom we all loved, can bind us.[50]

There is no evidence whether the Nashes replied, but at least the legal-financial problems were near a solution. Waldo outlined his debts as the basis of an appeal to Mr. Cutler, who advanced $200 and promised further help.[51] Finally,

YEARS OF THE WIDOWER

in May, 1834, Charles was able to tell William
that

> Waldo has received . . . 67 shares in the stock of the
> City Bank; 19 shares in Atlantick Bank, 31 shares in the
> Bost. & Rox. Mill Dam . . . & a balance of cash of be-
> tween 3 & 4000. . . . Well $11600 . .—on this he is to
> subsist, on the interest of it, for he gets but very little in-
> come now from any other quarter. The other ½ of Ellen's
> property . . . remains at present undivided & in Mr
> Cutler's hand.
>
> Now the interest of this 11600 . . will scarce sup-
> port both Mother & Waldo at the rate they live at. There-
> fore for the present we seem pretty nearly as poor as ever
> only Waldo does without a Profession.[52]

Waldo's view was more cheerful. After a long
paragraph to Edward about the superiority of
Reason to Understanding he added, "I am made
sure of an income of about $1200. wherewith the
Reason of Mother & you & I might defy the
Understanding upon his own ground, for the rest
of the few years in which we shall be subject to his
insults. . . . If you will come we will retreat into
Berkshire & make a little world of other stuff." [53]

By 1836 Waldo and at least Paulina Nash were
apparently on good terms, united, if by nothing
else, by disgust at the executor's delay.[54] But his
control of the money was almost over. The Court
entered a final decree in July, 1837, and before
the month was out Waldo had received $11,-
674.49 more from Ellen. He resisted investment
proposals from William: "As I hope to put my
leisure to high uses, I do not wish to put the good
deodand which secures it, at hazard." [55]

- 4 -

IMPORTANT THOUGH Ellen's family and estate were to Emerson in the first years after her death, his most absorbing concerns were the twin ones of what truth was his to communicate, and what channel of expression to choose. He must select his own "high uses." These were the years of crisis in his ministry and search for a new career, of old beliefs retested and new convictions affirmed. These parts of the period also wore tints of Ellen.

Waldo resigned from the ministry of the Second Church in September, 1832, the immediate cause being his liberal views of the meaning and administration of the Lord's Supper. His engagement to Ellen had preceded his ordination by three months; her death preceded his resignation by nineteen. Therefore there is some temptation to think that the prospect of marriage forced him into a professional commitment and that bereavement freed him to leave it. But that such circumstances "forced" him to or "freed" him from anything is hardly credible when related to the tenor of his whole life and other details of this period.

He had been moving steadily towards the ministry before he met Ellen—after all, he met her through a preaching engagement—and the most one might wish to say is that "under the incitement" caused by his engagement, "a good opportunity arising, he decided to accept a settlement." [56] As we have seen, Waldo himself had said that "ambition & curiosity" will prompt a young man of undeveloped ability "to prove by experiments the affections & faculties" he possesses.[57] Ellen tested his affections; the Second Church, his faculties. The two experiments were contemporary and parallel—both ended in sorrow and in growth—but one was not the sole cause of the other.

The theological and temperamental motives for Waldo's leaving the Second Church, voluminously recorded by him and his friends, publicly stated in his farewell sermon, and ably analyzed by many biographers, would almost certainly have driven him to resign even if Ellen had lived. Yet it is also true that when the crisis arose, his being a widower left him freer than otherwise to resign, and that just as her life had been a stimulus to him, her death left him significantly less interested in everything. Pervasive ennui, child of his grief, almost surely hastened a decision for which intellectual doubts and unfitness of temperament were the chief motives.

After his return from Europe he had some interest in a second ministerial settlement, but the prospect of Ellen's estate made it unnecessary that he search for a congenial congregation. Yet he was probably entirely accurate in the self-analysis of 1838 in which he said

I please myself with the thought that my accidental freedom by means of a permanent income is nowise essential to my habits, that my tastes, my direction of thought is so

strong that I should do the same things,—should contrive
to spend the best part of my time in the same way as now,
rich or poor. If I did not think so, I should never dare to
urge the doctrines of human culture on young men.[58]

- 5 -

MORE FORMATIVE than Ellen's relation to Waldo's ministry was her involvement in some of the
ideas he would preach in or out of a pulpit, partic-
ularly Compensation and immortality. These
ideas had, of course, relations to many other parts
of his life—relations which must be in the background while Ellen holds the stage.

Two months after Ellen's death Charles wrote
to William, "Here we are still alive & looking up
through the political & moral & social disasters of
life, like the grass through the snow, the greener
for being so visited." [59] He was expressing one of
Waldo's favorite ideas, Compensation. This took
several forms, but, generally, asserted that virtue
is rewarded, vice punished, suffering indemnified,
and joy paid for.[60]

As early as 1820, Waldo had written of

that eternal analogy which subsists between the external
changes of nature & scenes of good & ill that chequer human life. Joy cometh but is speedily supplanted by grief
& we look at the approach of transient adversities like the
mists of the morning fearful & many but the fairies are in
them.[61]

His conviction that "joy . . . is speedily supplanted by grief" underlay the fear, already

quoted from a letter to Aunt Mary, that he felt
soon after his engagement.[62] The same fear was
present, though outweighed by a contradictory
faith in God's continuous benefidence, when the
call to the Second Church was added to his other
blessings.

Whilst I enjoy the luxury of an unmeasured affection for
an object so deserving of it all & who requites it all,—I
am called by an ancient & respectable church to become
its pastor. I recognize in these events, accompanied as
they are by so many additional occasions of joy in the
condition of my family, . . . the hand of my heavenly
Father. This happiness awakens in me a certain awe: I
know my imperfections: I know my ill-deserts; & the
bounty of God makes me feel my own sinfulness the more.
I throw myself with humble gratitude upon his goodness.
I feel my total dependance. O God direct & guard &
bless me, & those, & especially *her,* in whom I am blessed.[63]

We do not know how Waldo's belief in Compensation and his theology of continuous beneficence
reacted when, two days later, this prayer was followed by Ellen's attack of bleeding—the one
which caused him to say she was "too lovely to
live long"; [64] but what had happened to her and
the remark he made seem to favor Compensation.

Both it and continuous beneficence supported
him during the shock of bereavement. His
immediate reaction to Ellen's death was of com-
pensating sorrow and joy, loss and gain, "The
past days the most eventful of my life are all a
dim confusion & now the pall is drawn over them,
yet do they shine brilliantly in my spiritual world.
Say, dear Aunt [Mary], if I am not rich in her

memory?" [65] This pattern he was frequently to
experience and frequently to expound: a loss in the
world of matter and affections compensated in the
world of spirit.

A journal passage of April, 1831, returns to
the beneficence of a God who is not only generous
but also consistent in pouring forth his gifts; yet
faith in an always generous grace is rather cautiously expressed: "I don't see but you may trust it
still." Much more confidence, based on experience,
permeates statements of June and August concerning the God of Balance.

Is not the law of compensation perfect? It holds as far as
we can see. Different gifts to different individuals but
with a mortgage of responsibility on every one. . . . I have
nothing charactered in my brain that outlives this word
Compensation.[66]

Compensations is one of the watchwords of my spiritual
world—& time & chance & sorrow & hope do not by their
revelations abate my curiosity.[67]

Having survived the test of Ellen's death, both
the Generous God and the God of Balance were
proof against all later storms, and both continued
important in Emerson's pantheon. But each un-
derwent a change—was transformed from a
Christian into a Transcendental concept and, to
oversimplify, from a deity into a law. In their new
forms they compose the two chief sections of
"Compensation" in the 1841 *Essays, First Series*.
The first part of the essay presents the Law of
Balance, "Every excess causes a defect; every defect an excess. Every sweet hath its sour; every

evil its good. . . . For every thing you have missed, you have gained something else; and for every thing you gain, you lose something." [68] But lest the doctrine of Compensation be mistaken as a "doctrine of indifferency," the second part of the essay describes the Generous God, now the Law of Growth: "The soul is not a compensation, but a life. . . . Neither can it be said . . . that the gain of rectitude must be bought by any loss. There is no penalty to virtue; no penalty to wisdom; they are proper additions of being," and the revolutions which accompany their influx are "in some happier mind . . . incessant." [69] Material advantages are kept in balance; in the mundane world nothing is given, everything is sold. But in the spiritual world, where self-reliance is God-reliance, a constancy in the flow of goodness, truth, and beauty can be trusted. It had been wrong to think that God might send a never-ending stream of honors, financial advancements, and romantic joys; it would not be wrong to expect a constant stream of insights gained partly from the droughts of that other stream.

Several passages of the early 40's let us trace Emerson's knowledge of compensations rather directly to Ellen's death. In one he says "We cannot let our angels go. We do not see that they only go out that archangels may come in." [70] It was a thought he expressed also in verses of "Give All to Love."

When half-gods go,
The gods arrive.[71]

Again, he wrote that "even the tragic and terrible are comely as they take their place in the pictures of memory. . . . Even the corpse that has lain in the chambers has added a solemn ornament to the house." [72] The most dramatic statement is in the final paragraph of "Compensation."

The death of a dear friend, wife, brother, lover, which seemed nothing but privation, somewhat later assumes the aspect of a guide or genius; for it commonly operates revolutions in our way of life, terminates an epoch of infancy or of youth which was waiting to be closed, breaks up a wonted occupation, or a household, or style of living, and allows the formation of new ones more friendly to the growth of character.[73]

Perhaps no other passage by Emerson attaches higher value to the law of spiritual growth—not, in this case, a growth for which no tax is paid, but one for which the tax remains less than the gain.

In this passage the only tax mentioned is the temporary sense of privation. Three years later another tax is revealed through a different context.

What opium is instilled into all disaster! It shows formidable as we approach it, but there is at last no rough rasping friction, but the most slippery sliding surfaces; we fall soft on a thought. . . . There are moods in which we court suffering, in the hope that here at least we shall find reality, sharp peaks and edges of truth. But it turns out to be scene-painting and counterfeit. The only thing grief has taught me is to know how shallow it is. That, like all the rest, plays about the surface, and never introduces me into the reality, for contact with which we would even pay the costly price of sons and lovers. . . . Souls never touch their objects. An innavigable sea washes with silent waves between us and the things we aim at and converse with. Grief too will make us idealists. In the death of my son, now more than two years ago, I seem to have lost a beautiful estate,—no more. I cannot get it nearer to me.[74]

Yet this passage is not to be accepted without qualification. The record seems clear that with Ellen's death in 1831, Emerson did feel "sharp peaks and edges" of grief, and did not "fall soft on a thought" until about three years later—when he made the statement, already quoted, that he had never keenly suffered. What he lacked by 1844 was an accurate memory of that earlier grief; perhaps by then he also lacked the ability to feel its equal.

In the sermon "Self-Culture," first preached in 1830, Emerson had said "Love, and you shall be loved." [75] He repeated the sentence in "Compensation." [76] Between the first and second uses occurred crucial events of his life. Compensation retained its truth through those years because its roots went down to the indescribable foundation of his personality. It gave him stability, but it had exacted a price. With respect to the burden one has to bear for acquiring external goods without labor (Was he thinking of Ellen's fortune?) Emerson could write "the gain is apparent; the tax is certain." But when he added, "there is no tax on the knowledge that . . . compensation exists," he should have remembered the emotional coin with which he had paid for the knowledge that even the death of loved ones is compensated.[77]

- *6* -

IMPORTANT IN changing the Christian *Lord* of
Balance to the Transcendental *Law* of Balance
was a divorce of Compensation from personal
immortality. Passages Emerson wrote before his
first marriage usually demonstrate a close link between Compensation and God's provision for our
personal survival. For example,

It is plain that in the present state this system [of punish-
ments and rewards] is not entire. There are griefs as the
loss of friends, the disappointment of parents in their
children, which do not admit of atonement in this world.
Here therefore is the burden of the proof; here is the sublime suggestion of futurity and a Providence that outlasts
time & connects the finite to infinity; the little & brief
concerns of men to the vast employments & natures of
Godhead & the Universe.[78]

After Ellen's death, however, the usual refer-
ence is to compensation of some sort in this life,
and the earlier theory even comes under explicit
attack: It is, he preached in 1832, "grossly defec-
tive to urge people to a good life because their
future well-being depends upon it. That is not the
right reason." [79] His meditations on the meaning
of Ellen's life and death had not proved there
were no compensations in an after-life, but had
proved that even the greatest losses experienced
here are also compensated here. Present life is a
"spiritual world" in itself, regardless of whether
a later and different one also exists, and in this

present life both spiritual and material compensations create a perfect harmony.[80] Both before and
after Ellen it was Compensation in which Emerson primarily believed; immortality had a second-
ary status supported by Christian revelation and
by the supposed necessity of a realm in which
accounts not balanced in this life could be rectified.
Almost simultaneously Emerson came to believe
both that all accounts are balanced here, and that
Christian revelation had been overvalued. Immortality was left sadly unpropped.

By the time of "Compensation" and its companion essay, "Spiritual Laws," there is nowhere
so much as a hint that compensations come in an
after-life or that there even is an after-life. Indeed, the balances are explicitly limited to this
world: Justice is "done now"; it "is not postponed." Admitting that we do not always observe
compensations, Emerson asserts that nevertheless
they exist now, within the secrecy of character.
Perhaps his own early practice is his target when,
in beginning the essay, he attacks a minister who
"urged from reason and from Scripture a compensation to be made . . . in the next life." He himself now appeals not to scripture but to nature,
hoping to show men "a ray of divinity, the *present*
action of the soul of this world." [81] Twenty-eight
years later his thought is the same.

There is a certain weakness in solemnly threatening the
human being with the revelations of the Judgment Day.
. . . An honest man would say, Why refer it? All that
is true and weighty with me has all its force now.[82]

Yet as several quotations have already shown, the chief source of Emerson's courage immediately before and after Ellen's death was the faith the two of them had in personal immortality. Both the frequency and the quality of his references to it show it in that crisis looming far larger than Compensation.

In 1829 Emerson preached "the Resurrection from the Dead," and Jesus as promising immortality; [83] he also assured Henry Ware that he considered the New Testament "the true record of the Revelation which established what was almost all we wanted to know, namely the Immortality of the Soul." [84] Ellen's death obviously made the matter more personal than it had ever seemed before. "Consolation for the Mourner" begins with "the truth of God brought by Jesus Christ," of which the "main fact is the immortality of the human soul." [85] Two weeks later Waldo asked in his journal,

Dear Ellen do you despise knowledge, or through holier organs does the soul fill her thirst & add to her appetite? Do you despise goodness? Oh no never here did you underrate a miser's mite, & not there, not there, my love. O suggest, coming from God's throne, suggest to this lone heart some hint of him. O forget me not, think with me pray with me.

Similar assurance of the fact (though not the precise form) of survival is expressed in poems and letters of that year. [86] Typical is the statement to Edward that "faith is strong—her faith stronger than death & the hope of heaven is more distinct to me by the aid of affection such as hers." [87]

In the journals for the last part of 1831, however, a weakening of confidence is suggested by the questions asked and the positions argued against.

Now my affections prophesy to me out of heaven where my angel is, & when I listen to them I do not fear death. . . .[88]

The day is sad, the night is careful, the heart is weighed down with leads. What shall he do who would belong to the Universe, "& live with living nature a pure rejoicing thing?" O friend, that said these words, are you conscious of this thought & this writer? I would not ask any other consolation than to be assured by one sign that the heart never plays false to itself when in its scope it requires by a necessity the permanence of the soul.[89]

The confidence publicly expressed was having its private trials, and the argumentative power of affection, twice mentioned, was wrestling with the processes Emerson distinguished as Reason and Understanding. In August of the next year the latter two were dominant.

When Jesus saith "he that giveth one of these little ones a cup of cold water shall not lose his reward," is not the best meaning [that the reward is] 'the love at which the giver has arrived'? . . . Through the N[ew]. T[estament]. there is not a just or grand thought but is made more round & infinite by applying it to the soul considered as the Universe living from God within."

A month later,

Don't tell me to get ready to die. I know not what shall be. The only preparation I can make is by fulfilling my present duties. This is the everlasting life.[90]

But no pattern of belief, consistent and constant, emerged. In December of 1834, Waldo rode to East Sudbury and reflected that

nature in the woods is very companionable. There, my Reason & my Understanding are sufficient company for each other. I have my glees as well as my glooms, alone. Confirm my faith (& when I write the word, Faith looks indignant.) pledge me the word of the Highest that I shall have my dead & my absent again, & I could be content & cheerful alone for a thousand years. . . .

The moment we indulge our affections, the earth is metapmorphosed; all its tragedies & ennuis vanish, all duties even, nothing remains to fill eternity with but two or three persons. . . . Were I assured of meeting Ellen tomorrow would it be less than a world [,] a personal world? Death has no bitterness in the light of that thought.[91]

When Charles died in 1836, Waldo wrote to Aunt Mary with confidence of Charles' personal continuance, but Waldo's supply of that faith was nearly exhausted.[92] "The Over-Soul" (1841) ridicules questions about the survival of personal identity and asserts that Jesus never "uttered a syllable concerning the duration of the soul."[93] mortality" (1861). Finally, the most personal of all evidence is that when young Waldo died in 1842, his father had neither expectation nor hope of seeing him again: "I comprehend nothing of this fact but its bitterness. Explanation I have none, consolation none that rises out of the fact itself; only diversion."[94]

Of the two ideas that most consoled Emerson at the time of Ellen's death, only Compensation stood the challenge of his later thinking; and it survived only in a form modified by the collapse of his faith in immortality. Ellen's death had forced brooding attention to both problems; the result would have disappointed her, for gradually, under the pressures of a weakening respect for tradition and an increasing allegiance to the present eternity of the Over-Soul, Waldo abandoned one faith that he and she had shared.

- 7 -

EMERSON LIVED fifty-one years after Ellen's death. Intensity of grief might have made him chronically suspicious of God's benevolence, turned him into a worshiper of the past, and kept him from a second marriage. That none of these reactions occurred is a tribute to his vitality, not evidence of callousness.

For his central ideas, his brief visit to the Jardin des Plantes in Paris in 1833, demonstrating the parallels which exist throughout nature, may have been more important than the whole of his first marriage; and his differences with Aunt Mary may have been more formative than his agreements with Ellen. Yet major aspects of his life were affected by her life and death. Her near relatives enlarged the circle of those he loved, her estate eased his professional life, her death may have quickened his leaving the ministry. His faith in personal immortality was tested; it survived only the period of his greatest need. His faith in

Compensation was modified, but in the long run strengthened. The emotional and intellectual bases of his optimism emerged stronger than ever, and sustained the rest of his life.

Nor is this, as we shall see, the whole of Ellen's influence. She left him reinforced in a high opinion of women, lonely, and again acutely aware both of his own shyness and of others' inability to meet his ideal of friendship. Yet he did marry again—and happily, even though Ellen's brilliance cast a shadow on the second Mrs. Emerson.

FIVE

Of Women and a Second Wife

"There is one birth & one baptism & one first
love and the affections cannot keep their youth
any more than men."

Emerson's Journal for February 13, 1831.

WHEN expounding Compensation, or describing
how he thought of Ellen's death several years
after the fact, Emerson provided striking evidence for those who accuse him of personal coldness; in journals and letters he sometimes accused
himself. But the complete public and private record is full of paradox created by varieties of
sincere moods, multiplicity of ideals and shifting
emphases among them, a refusal to simplify
falsely or systematize too soon. During the years
of his most mature writing he could say, on one
hand, that

there will be . . . [a] gulf between every me and thee.
. . . The universe is the [only adequate] bride of the soul.

All private sympathy is partial. Two human beings are like
globes, which can touch only in a point.[1]

On the other hand, he could also say that with

a friend . . . we are easily great. There is a sublime at-
traction in him to whatever virtue is in us. How he flings
wide the doors of existence! What questions we ask of him!
what an understanding we have! how few words are
needed! It is the only real society.[2]

Furthermore, when all the evidence from
Emerson's letters and journals, poems and essays,
actions and conversations, is arranged chronologi-
cally, and is then examined for evidence about his
alleged coldness, one gap appears: from the beginning of his engagement until his bereavement,
Waldo's one recorded loneliness was during his
absence from Ellen. Whenever in this period he
expressed a longing, it was not for an ideal companion who might never appear, but for the one
who had already met every demand. During his
first visit to New Concord—before the engagement, of course—he described to Charles what a
perfect friend might be, then added: "My quarrel
is with my race which will not give me what I
want, either in the shape of man or woman." He
had just met the person through whom the race
was to redeem itself. When, in Rome, after his
bereavement, he thought back to her, it was to
realize that an ideal companion "is never to dawn
upon me like a sun-burst. . . . Yet I saw Ellen at
once in all her beauty & she never disappointed me
except in her death." [3]

The only hints of there having been less than a perfect relation between them appear after her death. The first is minor: Waldo remembered, five months after Ellen died, that she "wondered why dearest friends even husband & wife did so little impart their religious thoughts." Yet the passage goes on to affirm the fulness of communication he had lost: "I sit alone from month to month filled with a deep desire to exchange thoughts with a friend who does not appear—yet shall I find or *refind* that friend?" [4]

Other pieces of evidence are perhaps more than hints, yet they point at least as much towards a supersensitive conscience and an imaginative memory as towards any real imperfection in Waldo's and Ellen's relation. For example, in the fulness of his grief five days after her death he wrote "I have no deserts like yours, no such purity, or singleness of heart. . . . Spirits are not deceived & now you know the sins & selfishness which the husband would fain have concealed from the confiding wife." [5] More significant is a journal entry of 1838 in which Emerson writes of recalling "all that delicious relation" of his first marriage, and of feeling

as ever how many shades, how much reproach. Strange is it that I can go back to no part of youth [,] no past relation [,] without shrinking & shrinking. Not Ellen, not Edward, not Charles. Infinite compunctions embitter each of those dear names & all who surrounded them. Ah could I have felt in the presence of the first, as now I feel my own power & hope, & so have offered her in every word

& look the heart of a man humble & wise, but resolved to
be true & perfect with God, & not as I fear it seemed, the
uneasy uncentred joy of one who received in her a good—
a lovely good—out of all proportion to his deserts, I might
haply have made her days longer & certainly sweeter &
at least have recalled her seraph smile without a pang.[6]

(Emerson's sense of insufficient merit was expressed during Ellen's lifetime, as we have seen,
to Aunt Mary. No doubt it was expressed also to
Ellen, but no evidence suggests that it decreased
her joy in marriage.) "I console myself," Waldo
continues,

with the thought that if Ellen, if Edward, if Charles could
have read my entire heart they should have seen nothing
but rectitude of purpose & generosity conquering the super-
ficial coldness & prudence. But I ask now why was not I
made like all these beatified mates of mine *superficially*
generous & noble as well as *internally* so? They never
needed to shrink at any remembrance; & I at so many sad
passages that look to me now as if I had been blind & mad.
Well O God I will try & learn, from this sad memory to
be brave & circumspect & true henceforth & weave now a
web that will not shrink. This is the thorn in the flesh.[7]

As we have seen, Charles sometimes found his
brother too busy for leisurely conversation, and
too absorbed in Ellen to give full attention elsewhere. And Ellen, in Philadelphia, sensed Waldo's anxiety to be back in Boston. But—if such
things can be measured—his remorse may well
have been disproportionate to its cause. Certainly
his son thought so: three years after the long
entry just quoted, many of its emotions and even

of its words—*delicious relations, shrink, infinite compunctions embitter*—appeared in the essay "Love"; in editing the passage the younger Edward Emerson commented that

although Mr. Emerson did not allow his mind to revert, looking ever to the brightness before, yet when, of a sudden, a memory came over him of his young wife, his brothers, his mother, gone from this life, he would, for the moment, start and moan, wrung by "infinite compunctions," due to his own tenderness and humble rating of himself, not thinking how they had prized him.[8]

Whatever needs to be explained about these moments of remorse or about Waldo's coldness—often exaggerated by him and by others—can largely be accounted for by his energy in extrapolating ideals and by the intensity of his relation to Ellen. A virtuoso pianist often denigrates his ability, even though it far surpasses the average; a man sensitive to what friendship can be, sees the poverty of mankind's usual contacts—and even of its exceptional ones. Then too, the actual love between Waldo and Ellen made every subsequent relationship fall short not just of an extrapolated ideal, but of an ideal once realized. He confessed that a vice of his constitution was "an excessive desire of sympathy";[9] from friends and other relatives he received much, but never again enough to satisfy his nearly insatiable longing based on an unrepeatable experience. Such considerations, and the facts of Waldo's biography, almost turn this passage from *Nature* (1836) into autobiography.

We are associated in adolescent and adult life with some friends, who, like skies and waters, are coextensive with our idea; who, answering each to a certain affection of the soul, satisfy our desire on that side; whom we lack power to put at such focal distance from us, that we can mend or even analyze them. . . . When much intercourse with a friend has supplied us with a standard of excellence, and has increased our respect for the resources of God who thus sends a real person to outgo our ideal; when he has, more-over, become an object of thought, and, whilst his char-acter retains all its unconscious effect, is converted in the mind into solid and sweet wisdom,—it is a sign to us that his office is closing, and he is commonly withdrawn from our sight in a short time.[10]

- 2 -

THE INTENSITY of first love fixed in Waldo's mind not only an ideal of companionship, but also an ideal of womanhood that Ellen fulfilled.

In his late thirties he thought that

a highly endowed man with good intellect and good con-science is a Man-woman and does not so much need the complement of woman to his being as another. . . . Her-maphrodite is . . . the symbol of the finished Soul.[11]

In his late forties he desired to exclude women from the Town and Country Club; [12] and with respect to Women's Suffrage he confessed,

whilst I should vote for every franchise for women, . . . if women asked, or if men denied it . . . I should not wish women to wish political functions, nor, if granted assume them. I imagine that a woman whom all men would feel to be the best, would decline such privileges if offered, & feel them to be obstacles to her legitimate influence.[13]

Except for the ambiguous matter of the Town and Country Club, these comments were, in Emerson's context, only praise for women; and he often praised them more than men: their agreement is the best authentication of a proposal involving ethics; they know their duty much better than men could describe it; they are a civilizing influence worthy of all admiration.[14] Two panegyrics have clear links to Ellen, one specifying that she, "in a life of solitude was incapable of an inelegance," the other asking

Is not affluence or at least easy circumstances essential to the finish of the female character—not to its depth & resources perhaps but to the *beauty* of mind & manners? Is it not because woman is not yet treated properly but some taint of Indian barbarity marks yet our civilization? She was made not to serve but to be served & only wealth admits among us of that condition.—Or is it that an eye to interest is a fatal blot to the female character & the poor scarce can help it?[15]

- *3* -

A MORE pragmatic affirmation of women's value came early in 1835, probably on January 30, when Emerson became engaged to Lydia Jackson—no relative of Ellen's physician.[16] There were some minor parallels to Ellen: riding lessons in the same class years earlier, a history of lung trouble, and the way of meeting—this time it was a lecture trip to Plymouth that made the two acquainted.[17] But the differences were more numerous.

In terms of Emerson's youthful imagery, Lidian, as he called her, may have been a fairy emerging from the mist, but she was no archangel to whom angel Ellen had fortunately yielded; [18] his compensation for the loss of Ellen was never Lidian, but "a thought." [19] Ellen had been eight years younger than Waldo; Lidian, now thirty-two, was eight months older. Waldo's mother regarded this "as a Petruchio sort of affair"; [20] Charles, who had praised Ellen's beauty, said that Lidian "is not beautiful anywise that I know, so you look at the outside alone," but he liked "her transparent character" and described her as "a sort of Sybil for wisdom." [21]

Waldo called her both "Sybil" and "Asia"—also "Queen," but the title never meant what it had when applied to Ellen.[22] His first letter after their engagement told Lidian that

in this new sentiment that you awaken in me . . . what might scare others pleases me, its quietness, which I accept as a pledge of permanence. I delighted myself on Friday with my quite domesticated position & the good understanding that grew all the time, yet I went & came without one vehement word—or one passionate sign. In this was nothing of design, I merely surrendered myself to the hour & to the facts. I find a sort of grandeur in the modulated expressions of a love in which the individuals, & what might seem even reasonable personal expectations, are steadily postponed to a regard for truth & the universal love. Do not think me a metaphysical lover. I am a man & hate & suspect the over refiners, & do sympathize with the homeliest pleasures & attractions by which our good foster mother Nature draws her children together. Yet am I well pleased that between us the most permanent ties should be the first formed & thereon should grow whatever others human nature will.[23]

In 1828 Waldo had praised idle sauntering and
anticipated finding a friend who would share his
delight; [24] now he told Lidian merely that "a sun-
set, a forest, a snow storm, a certain river-view,
are more to me than many friends & do ordinarily
divide my day with my books. Wherever I go
therefore I guard & study my rambling propensi-
ties with a care . . . of my high calling" as a poet.
To his brother William, he was even more explicit: I announce my engagement, he wrote, "in a
very different feeling from that with which I entered my first connexion [.] This is a very sober
joy. This lady is a person of noble character
whom to see is to respect. I find in her a quite
unexpected community of sentiment & speculation,
& in Plymouth she is dearly prized for her love &
good works." [25] Miss Jackson visited Waldo and
his mother in March of 1835; [26] three days after
her departure he wrote, though not explicitly because of her, "I come back to my rare book scarce
a journal. There is nothing so easy as to form
friendships & connexions. Yet lies there unseen a
gulf between every man & woman, & a Tragedy is
the protection of what seemed so helpless." [27]

Ellen's money eased Lidian's outward life; her
continued presence may not always have soothed
Lidian's spirit. Waldo gave Ellen's diamond to
Lidian, "and had it set, as she requested, in a
pin"; the jeweler, with unconscious symbolism,
misunderstood the instructions and made the
jewel useless.[28] Referring to a letter now lost,
Waldo told Lidian that her "dark eyes could not

read clearly the sentence about recent love
wounds. That word *recent* only respected the long
past, it did not touch the present. And whatever I
said, referred to some page or pages of my Day
Book where is most pompously recorded the hom-
age its author paid to bright village eyes. Will you
not honor me, my sybil, by visiting my lowly study
& reading the page." [29]

If Lidian accepted the invitation, did Waldo
show her the tribute, only a year earlier, to his
brilliant visions of "Ellen's beauty & love &
life"? [30] or the affirmation, just seven weeks after
the engagement to Lidian, "I loved Ellen, & love
her with an affection that would ask nothing but
its indulgence to make me blessed"? In the late
summer he made the entry, "I know no truer poetry in modern verse than Scott's line, 'And sun
himself in Ellen's eyes.' " [31]

Between January 30 and mid-September of
1835, Emerson's *Journal* contains these two important tributes to Ellen, but no significant refer-
ence or allusion to Lidian whom he married on
September 14, 1835.

- *4* -

IN JULY of this second engagement Emerson
bought the commodious Coolidge house in Concord, Massachusetts, and to it he brought Lidian
the night after their wedding. [32] Edward was now
dead; instead of retreating with him to Berkshire
as he had once wanted to do, Waldo retreated

with Lidian to fields which all the brothers had known intimately. Ellen had not known Old Concord so well, but how could she be kept away? "In this my new house," wrote Waldo, "no dead body was ever laid. It lacks so much sympathy with nature." [33]

Lidian may not have seen that ghost, but others she could not avoid. In 1838, her husband wrote to her about the death of one of his first wife's relatives, Ellen Tucker Washburn, whom, he said, "I used to love to see, & have blamed myself for neglecting lately." [34] Shortly after, he had a "remembering talk with Lidian" in which he went back to Ellen's first smile and "all that delicious relation." [35] In New Hampshire he travelled with Ellen's stepbrother.[36] In 1839,

24 February at 8 o'clock, a daughter was born to me [not "Lidian" or "us"]. . . . Lidian, who magnanimously makes my gods her gods, calls the babe Ellen. I can hardly ask more for thee, my babe, than that name implies. Be that vision, and remain with us, and after us.[37]

The resemblance was increased by using Tucker as the middle name. Perhaps Lidian was anxious to pay a tribute to the first wife, about whom she had heard so much praise; perhaps she sought to divert some of the father's emotion from a rivaling memory to a shared offspring. If the latter was her motive, she hardly succeeded.

While Emerson was connected with *The Dial* between 1840 and 1844, he published in it Ellen's poem beginning "Love scatters oil," and her "The Violet," as well as two poems by himself to El-

len—but none to Lidian.[38] When his first volume
of verse appeared in 1847, it contained these and
additional poems to Ellen—but again none to Lidian.

In his essay "Love" (1841), he said that "a
beauty overpowering all analysis or comparison
and putting us quite beside ourselves we can sel-
dom see" after age thirty; Lidian could have
quickly counted that her husband was twenty-
seven when he lost Ellen, thirty-two when he married again. The essay is lyric when dealing with
youthful romantic love, and some of its details
have explicit parallels to Waldo's years with his
first wife. It goes on to say that after a period of
marriage, husband and wife "resign each other
without complaint to the good offices which man
and woman are severally appointed to discharge
. . . , and exchange the passion which once could
not lose sight of its object, for a cheerful disen-
gaged furtherance, whether present or absent, of
each other's designs." [39] Perhaps only a sentimental wife would be hurt by that, but Lidian read, in
the next essay, that the finest friendship "leaves
the language of love suspicious and common" [40]—and there was no evidence that she and
Waldo shared the finest friendship. Lidian could
no doubt be happy in Waldo's publicly expressed
high opinion of women; she was extraordinary if
his public references to intense love pleased her
equally.

Many other parts of Emerson's works may also
have disappointed Lidian though a sensitive wife

of any prolific author may have equal experiences. He believed, for example, that "true love transcends the unworthy object . . . the poor interposed mask." [41] Twenty-five years after his own second marriage he told the world that "we are not very much to blame for our bad marriages. We live amid hallucinations; and this especial trap is laid to trip up our feet with, and all are tripped up *first or last"*—in a *first or later* marriage did he mean? [42] He may at moments have felt guilt as well as qualifications about his tie to Lidian, for he also advised that "art is a jealous mistress, and if a man have a genius for . . . poetry, . . . or philosophy, he makes a bad husband and an ill provider, and should be wise in season and not fetter himself with duties which will embitter his days and spoil him for his proper work." [43]

Some evidence of Emerson's implicit evaluation of his second marriage and continued devotion to Ellen may never have come to Lidian's eyes. One journal passage exults in going out of doors on a chill night of full moon: instantly "you leave far behind all human relations [,] wife, mother, & child [he had all three at the time], & live only with the savages—water, air, light, carbon, lime, & granite." [44] Only a little later, again in the journal, "I saw clearly that if my wife, my child, my mother, should be taken from me, I should still remain whole, with the same capacity of cheap enjoyment from all things. I should not grieve enough, although I love them. But could I make them feel what I feel,—the boundless resources of the soul . . . I should then dismiss forever the little remains of uneasiness I have in regard to them." [45] The wisdom of Compensation that he had learned from Ellen's death was controlling his emotions towards Lidian.

References to a still intense love for Ellen—references such as occurred during the engagement to Lidian—continue in the private record after their marriage. Lidian was a bride of two months when her husband was sufficiently moved to write about "the charming beauty which a few years ago shed on me its tender & immortal light. She needed not a historical name nor earthly rank or wealth. She was complete in her own perfections. She took up all things into her & in her single self sufficed the soul." [46] Four years later came another tribute; was it stimulated by a contrast with Lidian?

Ellen was never alone. I could not imagine her poor and solitary. She was like a tree in flower, so much soft, budding, informing beauty was society for itself, and she taught the eye that beheld her why Beauty was ever painted with loves and graces attending her steps.

When, after seven and a half years of his second marriage, Emerson expressed gratitude for "the bright revelations" of woman's "best nature" that had been made to him, it was not Lidian whom he cited as his teacher, but "the angel who walked with me in younger days." [47]

How much Lidian was moved by what she knew and what she may have surmised about her

husband's love is clearest from a pair of letters he
sent her from England in 1848. Her letters are
lost, but the reproaches in one are outlined by his
reply.

Ah you still ask me for that unwritten letter always due, it
seems, always unwritten, from year to year, by me to you,
dear Lidian . . . always due & unwritten by me to every
sister & brother of the human race. . . . It must content
you for the time, that I truly acknowledge a poverty of
nature, & have really no proud defence at all to set up, but
ill-health, puniness, and Stygian limitations. . . . Besides
am I not, O best Lidian, a most foolish affectionate good-
man & papa, with a weak side toward apples & sugar and
all domesticities, when I am once in Concord? . . . Well
I will come again shortly and behave the best I can [.]
Only I foresee plainly that the trick of solitariness never
never can leave me.

His second letter, six weeks later, again suggests
what stimulus Lidian had provided: she had been
reading a file of Ellen's letters, and had read them
generously. She sent balm to Waldo, but he may
have returned only salt for the wound that her
earlier letter had already revealed: Ellen's letters

deserved all you have said. For they came out of a heart
which nature & destiny conspired to keep as inviolate, as
are still those three children of whom you send me such
happy accounts. But I am deeply gratified by your pleasure & sympathy in them. Ah how we wander from goal to
goal of our life, and often it seems as if one thread of
consciousness did not tie the far parts together. Who am I
that roam these desarts, & knew this & that in old years?
But you should have seen Ellen. When she left this world,
I valued every body who had seen her, and disliked to meet
those who had not.[48]

- *5* -

SOME INCOMPATIBILITY between Lidian and
Waldo is part of the Emerson family tradition
and has been noted by other biographers. Lidian
did not share all her husband's religious convictions and sometimes satirized them; [49] she did not
provide the adoration, almost worship, with
which the youthful Ellen had flattered his shy
psyche.[50] Elizabeth Hoar may have irritated the
situation. No suggestion of impropriety has ever
linked her to Emerson, yet the facts invite a de-
cent speculation. She was engaged to Charles
Emerson before Waldo became engaged to Lidian, and the engagement lasted until Charles's
death in 1836. She never married, but continued
to live in Concord, very friendly with all the
Emersons, a frequent visitor in Waldo's home,
and an American whom he gladly met in Europe.
So frequent, admiring, and affectionate are his
references to her that one wonders what would
have happened if they had been Concord neigh-
bors when both were unengaged.[51]

Elizabeth's presence may have aggravated the
mild differences separating Waldo and Lidian. Ellen's presence certainly did, through the keen joy
of his memories, and through the touch of aloof-
ness which Ellen's death may have fastened on
him as a protection against pain and as a way of
living with the World Soul. It is not that Emerson
failed to love Lidian, but that he never stopped

loving Ellen more. We can surmise that Lidian
never expected Waldo to *forget* his "one first
love," but that she did hope he would in time love
equally the wife who was bearing and rearing his
children and sharing his daily life. But the two
loves were never equal.

- *6* -

WHILE EMERSON was on a western lecture tour in
1852 he wrote to his older daughter,

The beautiful Ellen Tucker, for whom you were named,
died twenty two years ago. Presently afterwards, her only
surviving sister Paulina went to Italy, with her husband,
& has lived in Leghorn & Pisa until now. Lately, she has
returned home, & now lives in Cambridge. . . . I have
written to her to give her joy on her return. But I should
like to send her a living letter. Do you not wish to take
the cars on the first fine morning, & go down to Cambridge, & find your way to her door, & say to her that your
father sends his love to her, & means to bring your mother
to see her as soon as he comes home. . . . Write on your
card Ellen L. Emerson [52] or better, Ellen Tucker Emerson.
Yes that is best, & send it up to her from the door. . . .
There is no necessity of staying any longer than just to
carry this friendly message.

Either young Ellen's visit or other means created
a complete reconciliation between Emerson and
Mrs. Nash; he told her during the Civil War that
"everything that touches you or your family will
always be exceptional to me, quite out of & above
the rule." [53]

The second Ellen probably received, upon the

death of Waldo's mother, the watch his first wife
had worn.[54] Jewelry was again symbolic, for as
her father grew increasingly forgetful in his last
years, this daughter who never married became
more and more his companion and support; they
traveled a great deal together—without Lidian—and she was one of several persons who
helped him prepare his last, rare lectures. Lidian
was frequently invited out during these late years,
played whist with the Alcotts, and became quite a
talker—at the same time that she imagined many
calamities. In intellectual matters, the younger
Ellen Tucker may have been closer to Waldo than
was his second wife.[55]

The last time that we know Emerson thought
of the first Ellen was in 1879, two and a half
years before his death. The Unitarian Church of
New Concord was celebrating its first half century
and asked Emerson to read a hymn composed by
George Kent.[56] Arriving on the day before the
ceremony, he went immediately to see the house in
which Ellen had lived and they had been married,
but could not find it. The next day Ellen's stepbrother took him to the house at its new location,
and Emerson saw the still familiar rooms. The
date the church had chosen for its celebration was
September 30. Emerson recognized the coincidence: he had been brought back to Concord ex-
actly fifty years after he and Ellen had there been
made man and wife.[57]

APPENDIX

A Touchstone for Biographies

Notes / Index

A Touchstone for Biographies

THE FOLLOWING REMARKS are a sampling rather than an exhaustive account of how Ellen Tucker has fared with her husband's biographers.

Not only did Ellen die young and after a brief marriage in which there were no children; she was the wife of a man then of only local reputation. She is not, therefore, known to us through the records of disciples, friends, and visitors who, attracted by the later Sage of Concord, left at least brief notes about his second wife. Her few surviving letters were as late as 1939 not available even to scholars,[1] and the first publication of Emerson's journals omitted some important passages concerning her.[2]

What little information was available was often ignored or distorted by the biographers. Most have been sufficiently chivalrous to mention Ellen's name and to report that her marriage was brief; few have said more than that. Five have been so discourteous as to give the wrong year for her death;[3] one of these is Oliver Wendell Holmes, who in the 421 pages of his *Ralph Waldo Emerson* (1884) refers to Ellen in only two sentences;[4] another is Alexander Ireland, a British biographer unable to control his aspirates, who wrote about *Helen* Louisa Tucker.[5] Moncure D. Conway would have us believe that when Emerson was buried in Concord, his body was borne "to the higher ground [of Sleepy Hollow] where lay the bride so early lost."[6]

James E. Cabot, whose two-volume *Memoir of Ralph Waldo Emerson* (1887) was for half a century the standard biography, deals with the first marriage itself on parts of but four pages.[7] Richard Garnett said in his *Life of Ralph Waldo Emerson* (1888) that Ellen "faded so quickly out of life and all memories but her husband's, that little seems to be known of her beyond her remarkable beauty, her fatal delicacy of constitution, and her buoyant spirit" (p. 48). In his *Ralph Waldo Emerson* (1907), George Edward Woodberry was more interested in philosophy than in biography; according to him, "there were no events in . . . [Emerson's] life, except the one decisive step of leaving the church" (p. 182).

O. W. Firkins's biography appeared in 1915. He said, probably with some exaggeration concerning his second instance, that Emerson's "two great passions, so far as we can judge, were his love for Ellen Tucker and his grief for his son" (p. 112); and he wrote about the earlier of these passions with puckishness and romantic embroidery. For example, he tells us that Ellen was "very beautiful 'by universal consent' (as . . . [Emerson] curiously remarks, as if a referendum were germane to the case)" (p. 29), and that the effect of his engagement

on Emerson's mind is suggestive. He was bewildered, like one who suddenly wakes up in the midst of a fairy tale; he was courtly, holding his love off at an obsequious distance; and he was meek. Or, changing our figures a little, we might say that he was as glad and still and surprised as a young child on whose shoulder a bright moth or bird has unexpectedly alighted (pp. 30–31).

Firkins's comment that Waldo's grief at Ellen's death "took the form of a great mournfulness rather than of poignant anguish" (p. 37) fits some but not quite all the evidence now available.

Thirteen years later than Firkins's book came Robert M. Gay's *Emerson: A Study of the Poet as Seer* (1928). Its handling of the first marriage is flawed both by inaccuracies and by questionable interpretations. Among the inaccuracies are a repetition (p. 82) of E. W. Emerson's mistake (*Emerson in Concord*, p. 37) that Waldo did not visit New Concord between his first meeting Ellen and their becoming engaged; a garbled account (p. 82) of the trips Waldo and Ellen took during their engagement; and the assertion (p. 89) that two lines in Waldo's journal "comprise all of the immediate record" of Ellen's death. Among Gay's questionable interpretations is that in December, 1827, Emerson "seems promptly to have fallen in love" (p. 81).

In 1929 appeared Phillips Russell's *Emerson: The Wisest American* with its own imperfections. His account of Ellen's effect on her husband is imaginative, figurative—and almost slushy. His type of elaboration is suggested by this passage.

> Something unaccountable and strange is detectable in Emerson's attitude towards his first wife. In his numerous references to her and to their life together occurs none of the endearments, none of the pet names, which men spontaneously bestow on fragile and attractive women. He worshipped her, but from a distance; as if she were a goddess or angel who had graciously but temporarily lent her shining presence to his life. No closeness, no intimacy, is revealed in the tone of calm grief with which he wrote of her. She remained his "friend," his "beautiful friend," his "enchanting friend." He was incapable of speaking of her in more passionate terms, as he was incapable of passion itself (pp. 79–80).

Did Russell not take the pains to learn of the times when Waldo called Ellen "Queen," "Ellinelli," "Nelly," "Wifey," "girl," "my rose," "*amie*"? [8]

But Russell's life seems restrained beside one that appeared in its English translation the next year, and which does nothing to destroy the stereotype of Gallic sensuousness. Régis Michaud says in the Foreword to his *Emerson: The Enraptured Yankee* (1930),

> For each line . . . I could . . . give references. . . . I have neither embellished nor added anything. I have merely dramatized, trying to feel and to reproduce the movement, the very rhythm of Emerson's life (p. xvi).

A sample dramatization of "the very rhythm" goes this way.

> Twenty-five years old, the springtide of life, and the man of ice prided himself upon never having loved. So he in-

forms the imaginary readers of his *Journal*. He is a celibate, he has never been a lover. This defiance of Eros was going to bring on the vengeance of the little god, for with his blue eyes, his cello-like voice, his benignity, his air of thoughtless seduction, he had everything to please women . . . (p. 75).

In September [*sic*], 1827, Ralph Waldo met his Eloa . . . Ellen. She was beautiful and frail as a picture from a keepsake, with a riotous head of thick curls, great hungry eyes, a pretty nose, impeccable throat and neck, a perfect bosom, a wasplike waist. . . . What was he going to do with this lily, he who reproached himself for his coldness and his lack of cordiality? Let us not expect romantic effusions from him. He is too apathetic to feel passion (pp. 75–76).

Van Wyck Brooks's chatty *Life of Emerson* (1932) avoided the weaknesses of Firkins', Gay's, Russell's, and Michaud's studies, but at the expense of giving only six sentences to the whole of Ellen's life and influence (pp. 42 and 60). Seven years later, however, the condition of Emerson scholarship in general and of our knowledge of Ellen in particular improved dramatically through Ralph L. Rusk's splendid six-volume edition of the *Letters* (1939). Rusk knew of Ellen's letters, but was not allowed to consult them (I, 275); nor was he allowed to print from a letter to Paulina Nash a portion which dealt with strained relations between her and Emerson (I, 406). By the time of his definitive *Life of Ralph Waldo Emerson* (1949), Rusk was able to quote from Ellen's letters, and his account of her marriage is markedly superior to all the others—except that those who want the very words spoken by Ellen and Waldo just before they became engaged can find them and other intimate details imagined by Charlotte E. Keyes in *The Experimenter*, a biography for young people (1962).

Notes

All italics within quotations occur in the original readings, unless the contrary is noted.

In order to hold the number of notes to a minimum, a single note often contains the page numbers locating a series of quotations or details which are derived from a given source. In such notes, the page numbers are given in an order which corresponds to the use of evidence in the text.

The following abbreviations occur in the notes.

DOCUMENTS

H   Houghton Library of Harvard University, where many Emerson manuscripts have been deposited by the Ralph Waldo Emerson Memorial Association.

J   R. W. Emerson, *Journals,* ed. Edward Waldo Emerson and Waldo Emerson Forbes, 10 vols. (Boston and New York, 1909–14).

JMN   R. W. Emerson, *Journals and Miscellaneous Notebooks,* ed. Gilman, Clark, Ferguson, Davis, *et al.,* 6 vols. (Cambridge, Mass., 1960–66).

L   R. W. Emerson, *Letters,* ed. Ralph L. Rusk, 6 vols. (New York, 1939).

N   Notebook used first by George Tucker, then by Ellen; owned by the Ralph Waldo Emerson Memorial Association.

OFL   *One First Love: The Letters of Ellen Louisa Tucker to Ralph Waldo Emerson,* ed. Edith W. Gregg (Cambridge, Mass., 1962).

PR   Manuscript *Preaching Record* in H.

R   Ralph L. Rusk, *The Life of Ralph Waldo Emerson* (New York, 1949).

W   Manuscripts owned by Dr. Ethel Emerson Wortis.

Wo   R. W. Emerson, *Works,* Centenary Edition, 12 vols. (Boston, 1903–4).

YES   R. W. Emerson, *Young Emerson Speaks,* ed. Arthur Cushman McGiffert, Jr. (Boston, 1938).

MEMBERS OF EMERSON'S FAMILY

CCE   Charles Chauncy Emerson (brother of RWE)
EBE   Edward Bliss Emerson (brother of RWE)
ETE   Ellen Tucker Emerson (wife of RWE)
MME   Mary Moody Emerson (aunt of RWE)
RHE   Ruth Haskins Emerson (mother of RWE)
WE   William Emerson (brother of RWE)

ONE: Dangerous Neighborhood

1 *L,* I, 201–27.
2 *JMN,* III, 99 (cf. II, 410).
3 *JMN,* I, 94–95 (cf. II, 405).
4 *JMN,* II, 238–39, 217, 409, 309–10.
5 Daily stages between Boston and Concord were advertised in *The New Hampshire Patriot and State Gazette* on July 23, 1821, and Feb. 12, 1827.
6 PR.
7 *L,* I, 222, 333.
8 *L,* I, 222–25.
9 *JMN,* III, 100.
10 *OFL,* p. 1.
11 Nathaniel Bouton, *The History of Concord* (Concord, N. H., 1856), p. 595.
12 MS. in the Kent papers owned by the New Hampshire Historical Society; *The New Hampshire Patriot and State Gazette,* July 9, 1821.
13 *L,* I, 222.
14 *OFL,* pp. 172, 15, 173.

15 *L*, I, 222.

16 *JMN*, V, 456.

17 *L*, I, 256; *OFL*, pp. 20, 49.

18 PR; *YES*, p. 19.

19 *L*, I, 233–34.

20 PR; *L*, I, 235.

21 EBE to WE (6.10.28: W); *L*, I, 236. *R*, pp. 132–33, quotes a poem which Rusk attributes to RWE and which he assigns to June of 1828. Edith W. Gregg and I agree that the poem is not in RWE's handwriting; Mrs. Gregg informs me that Professor Alfred R. Ferguson concurs in our judgment. The poem was probably written into Ellen's album by another of her beaux.

22 *L*, I, 222 n, 236, 248.

23 *L*, I, 253, 251–52, 256.

24 *JMN*, III, 146–47 (cf. *Wo*, II, 173).

25 *L*, I, 256, 252.

26 *R*, p. 130; *OFL*, p. 15.

27 PR.

28 *L*, I, 254–55.

29 *J*, VI, 379.

30 *L*, I, 256, 259.

31 *R*, p. 519; *OFL*, pp. 175–76 and plate 2; *J*, II, facing p. 256.

32 *L*, I, 271; EBE to WE (4.25.29: W).

33 *ETE Verses* (H #144), pp. 11–12; *R*, p. 149.

34 David Greene Haskins, *Ralph Waldo Emerson* (Boston, 1886), p. 44; Edward Waldo Emerson, *Emerson in Concord* (Boston and New York, 1888), p. 39.

35 *OFL*, pp. 14, 32–33, 167, 173, 1.

36 Frank B. Sanborn, *Ralph Waldo Emerson* (Boston, 1901), pp. 29–30.

37 *OFL*, pp. 38, 51, 11–12.

38 *JMN*, III, 149.

39 *R*, pp. 133–34.

40 *R*, p. 134 (A tentative identification of one of Emerson's works, advanced by Ralph Thompson in "Emerson and *The Offering for 1829*," *American Literature*, VI [May 1934], 151–57, has been confirmed in *JMN*, II, 267); *JMN*, II, 410–11; *L*, I, 256.

41 CCE to WE (1.9.29: W).

42 *L*, I, 256.

43 *J*, II, 259–60.

44 *OFL*, pp. 15, 18; *JMN*, III, 149; *L*, I, 260.

45 RHE to CCE (1.20.29: H); EBE to MME (1.17.29: H).

46 EBE to WE (1.20.29: W; Edward says Ellen "has been attacked within a day or two"; evidence in *OFL*, pp. 36 and 179 also points to January 19 as the day of the attack); *J*, II, 260.

47 EBE to WE (1.20.29: W); *OFL*, pp. 188–89; Wm. A. Kent to "My dear Daughter" (5.22.27: MS. in New Hampshire Historical Society).

48 *R*, pp. 21–29.

49 *L*, I, 184, 227; also 229–30. Cf. EBE to WE (5.3.29: W), "So G. W. Adams & F. G. King are added to the many dead of Waldo's class.—May he be spared!"

50 CCE to WE (1.22.29: W).

51 *L*, I, 235, 259. Doctor Jackson (1777–1867) is the subject of a sketch in the *DAB*. He helped train Doctor Charles T. Jackson (1805–1880), brother of Emerson's second wife. CCE to WE (1.27.29: W), "The Doctor says nothing of the expediency of Miss Tucker's changing the climate for another."

52 *L*, I, 259, 262, 264, 270; EBE to WE (2.9.29, 3.11.29, 4.19.29: W).

53 *OFL*, p. 25; *Wo*, IX, 387–88. (The dates of composition are uncertain, but the spring of 1829 seems more probable than any other period.)

54 CCE to WE (3.12.29: W); EBE to WE (3.11.29: W); *L*, I, 266.

55 *OFL*, pp. 26, 29.

56 CCE to WE (6.15.29: W).

57 PR.

58 *OFL*, pp. 41–54.

59 *L*, I, 271–72.

60 *OFL*, pp. 72, 76–77. Cf. MME to RWE, 12? 1828: H: "You go [to Ellen] maybe at the peril of injuring her."

61 *L*, I, 275–81.

62 *JMN*, III, 159–62.

63 *L,* i, 275, 281, 267 n, 279, 278.

64 *OFL,* pp. 87, 90–95, 104.

65 *L,* i, 281–84.

66 *New Hampshire Patriot,* October 5, 1829.

67 *Proceedings at the Semi-Centennial Celebration of the
. . . Second Congregational (Unitarian) Church . . .*
(Concord, N. H., 1879), pp. 24–25; MS. Kent gene-
alogy in the New Hampshire Historical Society; City
Historical Commission, *History of Concord,* ed. James
O. Lyford (Concord, N. H., 1903), ii, 1079.

68 Standing at 24 South Spring Street, the house is owned
and occupied by Mr. and Mrs. Robert Beyer, who are
responsibly aware of the historical significance of their
home.

69 *L,* i, 286 mentions Edward's absence; William learned
details of the wedding from Charles' letter (see next
quotation); Bulkeley was living with and working for
Israel Putnam of Chelmsford (*L,* i, 252, 419).

70 CCE to WE (10.4.29: W).

TWO: Queen and King

1 *OFL,* pp. 105–6. In *OFL, passim,* is evidence of at
least 21 letters from Waldo to Ellen, eight in July
alone. None of his letters to her appears to have
survived.

2 Bouton, pp. 595–96.

3 *OFL,* pp. 59–61, 54, 56, 72, 93, 41, 104, 34, 90–94,
104.

4 *OFL,* pp. 44, 98.

5 *L,* i, 313–14; *OFL,* p. 137.

6 N; *OFL,* p. 40.

7 *OFL,* pp. 12, 27, 39–40; 20, 84, 104.

8 MME to RWE (3.11.29: H).

9 *L,* i, 259.

10 Letter to me, 7.5.61, from the Reverend Eugene B.
Navias, who was, in 1961, minister of the Unitarian
Church, Concord, N. H.; Ellen joined this church
on August 30, 1829.

11 The church journal records the gift, and that the first communion was celebrated July 19, 1829.

12 *OFL,* pp. 160, 36, 35, 38, 37, 43.

13 *Wo,* II, 151.

14 MME to ETE, but addressed to RWE (1.24 or 25.29: H).

15 J. R. Lowell, *Fable for Critics.*

16 *OFL,* pp. 60, 46, 58, 32, 29–30.

17 *OFL,* pp. 150, 191, 83, 35, 91, 52, 23, 43.

18 Edward Waldo Emerson makes the suggestion in *Wo,* VI, 410. Cf. *JMN,* II, 142–43, 178–79, 225–26, 236–37.

19 *OFL,* pp. 125, 111, 13, 135, 168, 32.

20 *OFL,* pp. 180, 26, 68, 190, 60, 103, 56, 62, 135, 103, 104, 162, 23, 35.

21 It is owned by Mrs. Edith W. Gregg, and is marked by a few pencil lines and a poem indistinctly copied on a fly leaf.

22 *OFL,* pp. 133, 15, 22.

23 *OFL,* p. 13 (cf. *J,* II, 460, where Emerson recommends *Charles V* also to Elizabeth Tucker, Ellen's cousin); *JMN,* I, 395.

24 *L,* I, 259, 326. In 1822 Emerson copied "To a Waterfowl" into one of his notebooks (*JMN,* I, 392–93).

25 *OFL,* pp. 45, 62, 132, 12, 65, 128, 78.

26 *OFL,* pp. 13–14, 103, 3.

27 N.

28 *OFL,* pp. 39, 51, 99–100, 12.

29 *L,* I, 259; *J,* VII, 357.

30 *OFL,* pp. 149, 161.

31 *OFL,* p. 153; punctuation added in next-to-last stanza, and spacing altered in last stanza.

32 *J,* VII, 357.

33 *OFL,* pp. 74, 106, 135.

34 N.

35 *OFL,* pp. 65, 80.

36 *L,* I, 272.

37 N.

38 *OFL,* pp. 15, 37, 50, 92, 96; *R,* p. 219.

39 *OFL,* pp. 74, 76; *L,* I, 282.

40 *OFL,* pp. 23, 57, 96, 154.

41 *L*, I, 272, 296.

42 *OFL*, pp. 41, 49, 90, 99, 174; 52, 60; 21, 19, 83.

43 *OFL*, pp. 59, 69, 13, 70.

44 *OFL*, pp. 89, 93; *L*, I, 276.

45 MS. Rhyming Journal, Springfield, Hartford, Philadelphia (H).

46 *OFL*, pp. 124 (which gives *perpetuated* instead of the *perpetrated* in *L*, I, 297 n), 134 (which gives *skittish*, whereas I read the MS. as *sluttish*).

47 *OFL*, pp. 3, 12, 14, 81, 157.

48 *L*, I, 259; *OFL*, p. 13; *L*, I, 275, 282; "At the Saturday Club."

49 *R*, p. 131.

50 *J*, II, 266; *JMN*, II, 356; III, 159-62.

51 *L*, I, 224-26; *OFL*, p. 37.

52 *OFL*, pp. 22; 72, 76; 11; 98.

53 *OFL*, pp. 97; 89, 45, 82; 53-54; 27, 52; 28, 78.

54 *Selections from Ralph Waldo Emerson*, ed. Stephen E. Whicher (Boston, 1957), p. 1.

55 CCE to EBE and WE (10.30.30: W).

56 *R*, p. 149.

57 "Emerson" (in *Partial Portraits*), reprinted in *Henry James: Representative Selections*, ed. Lyon N. Richardson (New York, etc., 1941), p. 136; Whicher in *Selections*, p. [ix].

58 *Wo*, IX, 109-10. Cf. Charles' complaints of Waldo's being too wrapped up in Ellen.

59 Phillips Russell, *Emerson: The Wisest American* (New York, 1929), p. 80.

60 *JMN*, III, 153.

61 Robert M. Gay, *Emerson: A Study of the Poet as Seer* (Garden City, N. Y., 1928), p. 83; *R*, p. 133.

62 *Wo*, IX, 99.

THREE: Winged for Flight

1 CCE to WE (10.4.29: W).

2 *L*, I, 285.

3 *L*, I, 286; Edward Waldo Emerson, *Emerson in Concord*, pp. 38-39.

4 R, pp. 142–44.

5 L, I, 289; CCE to WE (12.3.30: W).

6 CCE to WE (11.12.29: W), MME to CCE (10.10.29: H).

7 L, I, 270; 288, 290; 285.

8 OFL, pp. 112; *L*, I, 285.

9 JMN, III, 181.

10 Wo, IX, 94–95; *JMN*, III, 181–82. (The poem is dated December, probably 1829, in *Wo*, IX, 435, and 1830 in *J*, II, 293.)

11 L, I, 286.

12 OFL, p. 116.

13 MME to ETE and RWE (1.14.30: H).

14 Wo, X, 595.

15 OFL, pp. 116–17.

16 MME to EBE (3.15.30: H).

17 MME to RWE (4.6.30: H).

18 L, I, 293–95.

19 OFL, pp. 118–19.

20 L, I, 295.

21 OFL, p. 121. Spacing in original.

22 L, I, 296–97.

23 OFL, pp. 122–23.

24 L, I, 296–300; *R*, p. 145.

25 W. H. Furness to J. E. Cabot (9.29.82: H). Cf. *J*, II, 460.

26 L, I, 297–98.

27 OFL, p. 123.

28 L, I, 299.

29 OFL, p. 128.

30 L, I, 302; *Wo*, IX, 99.

31 Wo, IX, 93–94.

32 L, I, 302.

33 CCE to WE (5.28.30: W), CCE to EBE and WE (6.27.30: W).

34 CCE to WE and EBE (8.11.30 and 8.14.30: W).

35 EBE to WE (8.23.30: W).

36 L, I, 307.

37 PR.

38 CCE to WE and EBE (8.11.30; 8.14.30: W); CCE to WE (9.25.30; 10.1.30: W).

39 MME to RWE (8.30.30: H); *L*, I, 307.

40 EBE to WE (8.27.30: W).

41 CCE to WE (10.1.30: W).

42 *R*, p. 147.

43 *L*, I, 310, 302 n; *OFL*, p. 134.

44 CCE to EBE and WE (10.30.30: W).

45 *OFL*, p. 134.

46 CCE to WE (12.3.30: W).

47 CCE to RHE (12.11.30: W).

48 *OFL*, p. 136; *L*, I, 314.

49 CCE to MME (9.12.30: H).

50 CCE to EBE and WE (10.30.30: W).

51 *L*, I, 310–13.

52 *OFL*, p. 135. I read the MS. as giving & instead of ? after *Bostonians*.

53 *L*, I, 315.

54 *JMN*, III, 205.

55 RHE to EBE (12.21.30: H).

56 PR; *YES*, p. 268.

57 CCE to WE (1.6.31: W).

58 *OFL*, pp. 136–38.

59 *YES*, pp. 127–28.

60 RHE to EBE (1.27.31; 3.1.31: H).

61 PR; RHE to EBE (1.27.31: H).

62 *L*, I, 316.

63 RHE to EBE (1.28.31: H).

64 CCE to WE (1.30.31: W).

65 *L*, I, 317.

66 CCE to WE (2.6.31—the second of two letters of the same date: W).

67 RHE to EBE (3.1.31: H).

68 *L*, I, 321.

69 RHE to EBE (3.1.31: H).

70 CCE to WE (2.6.31—the first of two letters of the same date: W).

71 CCE to WE (2.6.31—the second letter: W).

72 CCE to MME (2.6.31: H).

73 CCE to WE (2.7.31: W).

74 *JMN*, III, 227–28.

75 *R*, p. 149.

76 RHE to EBE (3.1.31: H).

FOUR: Years of the Widower

1 *L*, I, 318.
2 RHE to EBE (2.11.31 and 4.19.31: H).
3 *JMN*, III, 253, 226–28.
4 *JMN*, III, 228–29, 285–86, 289–90.
5 *YES*, p. 243.
6 *YES*, pp. 139–44.
7 *L*, I, 319–22.
8 *L*, I, 332–33.
9 *JMN*, III, 227.
10 RHE to EBE (3.7.31: H).
11 *JMN*, III, 244.
12 *L*, I, 326.
13 *JMN*, III, 309.
14 Haskins, *Emerson*, pp. 44–45. Haskins says that the cemetery was "not devoid of natural attractions"; the visits to its natural beauty may have been the beginning of those almost daily rural and forest walks which marked Emerson's life from the 30's until close to his death.
15 *YES*, p. 143.
16 *JMN*, IV, 7. Rusk and Alfred R. Ferguson believe Emerson actually opened the coffin (*R*, p. 150; *JMN*, IV, xv), but cf. the dream recorded in *JMN*, III, 226.
17 *OFL*, p. 82.
18 CCE to EBE (3.12.31: H).
19 *J*, II, 367.
20 *JMN*, III, 257–58, 229 ff. One fragment (232) anticipates "Threnody," written after the death of Emerson's son, Waldo.
21 *JMN*, III, 230, especially n. 56.
22 *L*, I, 325.
23 *JMN*, III, 257–58.
24 *L*, I, 367–68.
25 *Wo*, IX, 396. Cf. 97: Ellen's "The Violet."
26 Moncure D. Conway, "Thomas Carlyle," *Harper's New Monthly Magazine*, LXII (May 1881), 899.
27 *Wo*, II, 81–82.

28 *JMN,* IV, 292, 263.

29 *L,* I, 319. With the repetition of *faithful* in the last sentence here, compare the repetition of *pleasant* (*L,* I, 332; *JMN,* III, 230), *sad* (*L,* I, 330), *When I think of you* (*JMN,* III, 275), *dearest Ellen* (*JMN,* III, 230), *not there* and *suggest* (*JMN,* III, 240). Such repetition may be associated in Emerson's style not only with emphasis, but also with wistfulness.

30 WE to RWE (6.12.31: W).

31 *L,* I, 324, 327, 330.

32 *L,* I, 332; RWE to EBE in postscript of RHE to EBE (8.10–18.31: H).

33 *L,* I, 332, 335.

34 *L,* I, 335, 337.

35 *JMN,* III, 303–4; *J,* II, 458–62.

36 CCE to WE (11.27.32: W).

37 *JMN,* IV, 60, 62.

38 *JMN,* IV, 64–65.

39 RHE to CCE (2.12.33: H).

40 *JMN,* IV, 72. A manuscript in the Kent collection of the New Hampshire Historical Society states that Mrs. Kent died at Concord (N. H.), February 28, 1833, aged 57. The place and her age are confirmed by *The Patriot,* March 11, 1833.

41 *JMN,* III, 97.

42 *L,* I, 323.

43 *L,* I, 327.

44 *L,* I, 345; *R,* p. 157.

45 *L,* I, 345, 349.

46 CCE to WE (5.17.32: W).

47 CCE to WE (12.3.32: W).

48 CCE to WE (1.14.33: W).

49 *L,* I, 401–2.

50 *L,* I, 405–6, supplemented by lines which Rusk omitted from the letter (RWE to Paulina Nash, 1.19.34: H).

51 CCE to WE (1.25.34: W).

52 CCE to WE (5.13.34: W).

53 *L,* I, 413–14.

54 CCE to WE (4.6.36: W); *L,* II, 66.

55 *L,* II, 86–87, 90, 92. In 1842 and 1843 Emerson received additional sums of $397 and $353 from Mr.

Cutler and from the estate of Ellen's brother George (*L*, III, 42, 224).

56 George E. Woodberry, *Ralph Waldo Emerson* (New York, 1926), p. 29.

57 *JMN*, II, 309.

58 *J*, v, 43.

59 CCE to WE (4.12.31:W).

60 Henry F. Pommer, "The Contents and Basis of Emerson's Belief in Compensation," *PMLA*, LXXVII (June 1962), 248–53. A belief in Compensation, especially the educative effects of evil, is expressed by Ellen in *OFL*, p. 2.

61 *JMN*, I, 19.

62 *J*, II, 258–60.

63 *JMN*, III, 149–50.

64 CCE to WE (1.22.29:W).

65 *L*, I, 318.

66. *JMN*, III, 249–50, 265–66.

67 *L*, I, 330.

68 *Wo*, II, 98.

69 *Wo*, II, 120, 122, 125.

70 *Wo*, II, 125.

71 *Wo*, IX, 92.

72 *Wo*, II, 131. There is a close parallel in *JMN*, v, 101.

73 *Wo*, II, 126. *JMN*, I, 147 (1822) provides an interesting way of judging Emerson's development. It emphasizes how one can grow as a result of changing scenes, leaving friends, breaking our domestic habits. It is a youth's anticipation of the experiences which were to validate and enrich the close of "Compensation."

74 *Wo*, III, 48. In Nathaniel Hawthorne's *The Scarlet Letter*, written after this passage (from "Experience") had been published, Pearl "wanted—what some people want throughout life—a grief that should deeply touch her, and thus humanize and make her capable of sympathy."

75 *YES*, p. 102.

76 *Wo*, II, 116.

77 *Wo*, II, 123.

78 *JMN*, III, 5–6; also 48; II, 149–50; *YES*, pp. 10 and 18. An exception occurs on *JMN*, III, 62.

79 *YES*, p. 245. The same idea appears also in *JMN*, IV, 41.

80 *L*, I, 318, 330.

81 *Wo*, II, 95, 102, 121, 94, 93; italics added.

82 *J*, X, 304.

83 *YES*, p. 35.

84 *L*, I, 273.

85 *YES*, p. 138.

86 *JMN*, III, 240, 289–90; *L*, I, 331–33.

87 *L*, I, 321.

88 *JMN*, III, 267–68. But an emphasis on *hopes* of immortality had appeared at least as early as 1.6.30 in RWE to Anne Jean Lyman (Susan Lyman Lesley, *Recollections of my Mother* [Boston and New York, 1899], p. 256).

89 *JMN*, III, 309.

90 *JMN*, IV, 39, 41.

91 *JMN*, IV, 359–60.

92 George Frisbie Hoar, *Autobiography of Seventy Years*, reprinted in *The Emerson Society Quarterly*, No. 16 (III Quarter, 1959), p. 3.

93 *Wo*, II, 283–84. "The full effect of Ellen's death on Emerson has yet to be examined. The evidence in these journals, much of it hitherto unpublished, suggests that her death played a large part in his rejection of orthodox Christianity" (*JMN*, III, xi). The earlier part of the paragraph is wholly about immortality. It must be remembered that many parts of orthodox Christianity Emerson had rejected years before he met Ellen: divine inspiration of Scripture, trinitarianism, etc.

94 *J*, VI, 166. Some lines of "Threnody" might, out of context, be taken as expressing at the time of Waldo's death a faith in immortality (*Wo*, IX, 148–58, ll. 35, 189–94, 268–69, 272–81, 288–89); but in the context of the poem and of Emerson's vocabulary and symbolism at that time, nothing in the poem argues, in my opinion, for the survival of personal identity. Note that in *L*, I, 330 (8.15.31) "every star that sinks on this rises in the other firmament," whereas in "Threnody" man approaches death "Star by star his world

resigning" (l. 165) without assurance that he will see those stars again.

FIVE: Of Women and a Second Wife

1 *Wo*, III, 77.

2 *Wo*, VI, 272.

3 *L*, I, 225, 376.

4 *JMN*, III, 272; italics added.

5 *JMN*, III, 226–27.

6 *JMN*, V, 456.

7 *JMN*, V, 456.

8 *Wo*, II, 171, 409.

9 *JMN*, IV, 91.

10 *Wo*, I, 46.

11 *J*, VI, 210, 378. Cf. *JMN*, III, 193, "There is no sex, in thought, in knowledge, in virtue."

12 Kenneth Walter Cameron, "Emerson, Thoreau, and the Town and Country Club," *The Emerson Society Quarterly*, No. 8 (III Quarter, 1957), p. 2.

13 *L*, IV, 230.

14 *J*, V, 460; VI, 378; X, 171–72. Parallel ideas appear in *J*, X, 99–100; *Wo*, III, 149–52; XI, 412.

15 *JMN*, IV, 300, 16.

16 *R*, p. 211; *L*, I, 434–36; *JMN*, V, 14 claims the engagement had occurred by January 23.

17 *R*, p. 219; *J*, III, 541; *R*, pp. 210–11.

18 *JMN*, I, 19; *Wo*, II, 125.

19 *Wo*, III, 48.

20 CCE to WE (9.14.35: W).

21 CCE to WE (2.12.35, 3.3.35: W).

22 *L*, I, 437, 438; *R*, p. 225 and notes; *L*, I, 434.

23 *L*, I, 434.

24 *JMN*, III, 136–37.

25 *L*, I, 435–36.

26 CCE to WE (3.3.35, 3.13.35: W).

27 *JMN*, V, 17. Note that both here and in the preceding quotation *connexion* occurs, presumably meaning *engagement* in both places. Six days after Lidian's departure, Waldo condemned Boccaccio for representing "as

frequent, habitual, & belonging to the incontinent"
those "pleasures of appetite which only at rare intervals a few times in a life-time are intense, & to whose
acme continence is essential" (*JMN*, v, 22).

28 *R*, p. 211.

29 *L*, i, 437.

30 *JMN*, iv, 263.

31 *JMN*, v, 19, 85. The line is paraphrased from *The
Lady of the Lake*, Canto vi, xxiv.

32 CCE to WE (9.14.35: W). The house still stands.
Emerson paid $3,500 for it (*R*, p. 223); in chapter
one of *Walden* (1854), Thoreau says that "an average
house in this neighborhood costs perhaps eight hundred
dollars."

33 *JMN*, v, 101. Cf. *Wo*, ii, 131, quoted above.

34 *L*, ii, 116.

35 *JMN*, v, 456.

36 *L*, ii, 146.

37 *J*, v, 166–67.

38 *The Dial*, i, (July 1840), 72; i (January 1841), 314;
iii (July, 1842) 73–74; iii (January 1843), 327–28.

39 *Wo*, ii, 174, 187.

40 *Wo*, ii, 201.

41 *Wo*, ii, 216.

42 *Wo*, vi, 316; italics added. Note the contrast to the
hopefulness cited in chapter one from *JMN*, ii, 217.

43 *Wo*, vi, 114.

44 *JMN*, v, 496–97.

45 *J*, v, 115.

46 *JMN*, v, 108.

47 *J*, v, 165; vi, 379. In *L*, ii, 397, RWE again refers (in
1841) to those closest to himself; he mentions MME,
CCE, EBE, and ETE—but not Lidian.

48 *L*, iv, 33, 54.

49 *R*, pp. 225–26; Whicher in *Selections*, p. 480.

50 "Most biographers think that Emerson was cold and
shy; this type of person often is most happy with an
immature person who will respect and adore him. . . .
One may wonder if the shy and cold Emerson needed
this immature and worshipping girl for his psyche."
—Leonard London in a student paper.

51 R, L, J, JMN, passim.

52 I accept Rusk's interpretation of the *L.* in Ellen L. Emerson given in *L,* IV, 338 n: "No doubt Emerson unintentionally wrote the second initial of the maiden name of Ellen Louisa Tucker, for whom he had named his daughter."

53 L, IV, 338; V, 384.

54 L, IV, 410.

55 R, passim, but especially p. 483.

56 Proceedings at the Semi-Centennial Celebration of the . . . Second Congregational (Unitarian) Church . . . (Concord, N. H., 1879), p. 3.

57 James Elliot Cabot, *A Memoir of Ralph Waldo Emerson* (Boston and New York, 1897), II, 679–80.

APPENDIX: A Touchstone for Biographies

1 L, I, 275.

2 Cf. *e.g., J,* II, 356 and *JMN,* III, 226–27.

3 George Willis Cooke, *Ralph Waldo Emerson: His Life, Writings, and Philosophy* (Boston, 1881), p. 34; Moncure D. Conway, *Emerson at Home and Abroad* (London, 1883), p. 59; Robert M. Gay, *Emerson: The Poet as Seer* (Garden City, N. Y., 1928), p. 84.

4 Oliver Wendell Holmes, *Ralph Waldo Emerson* (Boston and New York, 1884), pp. 55–56. (The edition of 1912 gives the same information about Ellen.)

5 Alexander Ireland, *Ralph Waldo Emerson: His Life, Genius, and Writings,* 2d ed. (London, 1882), p. 11.

6 Emerson at Home and Abroad, p. 8.

7 James Elliott Cabot, *A Memoir of Ralph Waldo Emerson* (Boston and New York, 1897), I, 146–48, 172.

8 L, I, 282, 283, 275, 317, 306, 316, 336; *JMN,* III, 195.

Index

30, 80, 86–87, 92, 94;
Compensation, 11, 68–
76, 79, 80, 81, 88, 94;
nature, 22, 51, 75, 78,
89, 91, 93, 116; immor-
tality, 50–53, 59, 60, 61,
68, 74–80, 83; woman's
suffrage, 86
—illness, 7, 12–13, 28, 35
—ministry, 7, 9, 12, 13, 14,
15, 16, 20, 31, 37, 44,
46, 47, 52, 56, 66–68,
79, 102. *See also* Preaching
—Phi Beta Kappa invita-
tion, 54
—preaching, 3, 5, 6, 7, 9,
10, 14, 35, 39, 42, 46, 47,
52, 67, 74
—reading, 17, 35
—travel: Europe, 54, 57–
58, 61, 64, 67, 79, 82,
95, 96; New England,
15, 16, 42, 55, 65, 91;
Philadelphia, 29, 36–40,
41, 84; South Carolina
and Florida, 12, 15
—works: Rhyming Jour-
nals, 15, 28–29, 30, 37–
39; "Spiritual Laws,"
21, 75; "Initial, Dae-
monic, and Celestial
Love," 32; "Thine
Eyes . . . ," 33, 40;
"And Ellen . . . ," 35;
"To Ellen at the South,"
40–41; "Consolation for
the Mourner," 46, 52–
53, 54–55, 76; "Self-
Reliance," 58; *Essays,
First Series,* 70; "Com-
pensation," 70, 72, 73,
75; "Give All to Love,"
71; "Self-Culture," 73;

"Immortality," 78;
"The Over-Soul," 78;
Nature, 85; "Love," 85,
92; "Threnody," 116,
119
Emerson, Ruth Haskins (d.
1853, mother of RWE),
3, 12, 14, 42, 44, 47, 51,
54, 61, 65, 88, 89, 98
Emerson, Waldo (1836–
42, son of RWE), 78,
102
Emerson, William (1801–
68, brother of RWE):
3, 11, 12, 13, 17, 19, 30,
31, 35, 45, 53, 62, 65,
89; letter cited, 59
Emerson, William (1769–
1811, father of RWE),
12

Farnhams, 44
Firkins, O. W., 102–3
Furness, William H., 39

Garnett, Richard, 102
Gay, Robert M., 103
Gift books, 8, 10

Harvard College, 3, 6, 7,
13, 62
Hoar, Elizabeth, 96
Holmes, Oliver Wendell,
30, 101

Ireland, Alexander, 102

Jackson, Charles T.
(brother of Lydia Jack-
son), 110
Jackson, James, 13, 14, 28,
43–44, 47, 87
Jackson, Lydia (also Lid-
ian), 80, 87–98